DATE DUE

S

MAR 2 9 2006		
APR 1 8 2006		
MAY 2 2 2006		
JUN 2 7 2006		

GAYLORD   PRINTED IN U.S.A.

Finland

Finland

BY SYLVIA MCNAIR

Enchantment of the World
Second Series

Children's Press®

A Division of Grolier Publishing

NEW YORK   LONDON   HONG KONG   SYDNEY
DANBURY, CONNECTICUT

This book is lovingly dedicated to the people
who have always made my life an exciting adventure:
Allen, Donald, Roger, and Patricia.

Consultant: Börje Vähämäki, Ph.D., Professor of Finnish Studies,
University of Toronto, Ontario, Canada

Please note: *All statistics are as up-to-date as possible at the time of publication.*

Library of Congress Cataloging-in-Publication Data

McNair, Sylvia.
Finland / Sylvia McNair.
p. cm. — (Enchantment of the world. Second series)
Includes bibliographical references and index.
Summary: Describes the geography, plants, animals, history, economy, language,
religions, culture, sports, arts, and people of Finland.
ISBN 0-516-20472-6
1. Finland—Juvenile literature. [1. Finland.] I. Title. II. Series
DL1012.M35 1997
948.97—dc21   97-4972
                                                                              CIP
                                                                              AC

Acknowledgments

The author gratefully acknowledges the assistance and encouragement of the following people: Ritva Muller of the Finnish National Tourist Board in New York; Fred Niemi, Finnish Consul for Chicago; Michael Loukinen of the FinnFest USA '96 Committee; and the following people who made my visit to Finland so enjoyable and informative—Irmeli Torssonen, Lena Sarlin, Ann-Karin Koskinen, Anja Saaristo, Marjatta Kulku, and Kaarina Pelkonen. Also, thanks to Allen McNair, Dixie Franklin, Gregory Hokans, and especially Anna Idol, who helped me get the job done.

Cover photo:
Traditional Sami
folk clothing

Contents

The midnight sun over Helsinki, Finland

Welcome to Finland

Few people anywhere enjoy the outdoors as much as the Finns, who live in a country in northern Europe known for its beauty. Families who live in cities rush to the countryside as often as they can. In summer they head for one of Finland's thousands of lakes or islands to swim or boat or fish. They hike in the forests and pick berries and mushrooms.

The sun almost forgets to set on summer nights in Finland, and people cut their sleeping hours short. After all, winter is coming, when it is cold and dark most of the time. There's plenty of time for sleeping then.

B
UT EVEN IN WINTER THE OUT-
doors beckons Finns. Nearly
every town has a skating rink
and a ski jump. A world-famous
marathon race attracts more
than 10,000 cross-country skiers
each year.

A bicycler enjoys a sunny day by one of Finland's beautiful lakes.

Finnish designers, admired all over the world, often use themes from nature, such as birds, plants, and clouds. Nature is not viewed as a hostile force, but as a source of enjoyment, inspiration, and strength.

If you ask a Finn to list the outstanding qualities of the people of this land, you'll be told: "We love nature. We love sports. We work hard and play hard. We're somewhat shy and reserved. You can depend on a Finn to be trustworthy and tell it like it is. We have *sisu*, and we all love the *sauna*." And just what do those two Finnish words mean?

It is said that Finns are hard-working and trustworthy.

Sisu (SI-su) means courage, tenacity, endurance, a special strength and determination

Geopolitical map
of Finland

not to give up in the face of obstacles. It may also be translated as "guts," or "stubbornness beyond all reason." Finns use the word proudly to describe their national character, their ability to meet difficult challenges. Sisu helped the ancient Finns deal with a harsh climate. More recently, it helped Finns survive invasions and wartime occupation by foreign powers.

Most of all, sisu has been an important factor in the rapid development of this small country. Since it became an independent nation only about eighty years ago, Finland has made giant strides. It began as a country where nearly everyone earned a living from forests, farms, or fishing. Today, it is one of the most technologically advanced nations in the world.

Sauna (SOW-nah) is a Finnish word known all over the world. Simply translated, it means "steam bath," but to Finns the sauna is much more. It is a tradition more than two thousand years old. It is a ritual, a recreational activity, and a social meeting place.

In rural Finland, the sauna is a small, one-room, wooden building set apart from the house. In a sauna, stones are heated on top of a wood-burning stove or *kiuas* (KEE-yoo-ahs). When the stones are very hot, water is thrown over them to produce a fine vapor called *löyli* (LOH-ee-lee) that fills the small room.

On average, the air temperature in the room is between 170°and 200°F (75° and 90°C). The purpose is to stimulate perspiration. Small, wet birch switches or *vihta* (VI-tah) are used to pat the skin—gently or vigorously. This process creates a pleasant perfume and helps the blood to circulate.

A smoke sauna with *vihta*, or branches used to stimulate the skin

The next part of the ritual is cooling down, usually by taking a cold shower or jumping into a cool lake. During the winter months, many people cut holes in the ice on a lake so they can plunge into the water. They usually repeat the cooling process several times. Afterward, each person dries off slowly, trying not to stimulate the blood further by rubbing. After dressing, they share a friendly drink and snack.

An old Finnish proverb says, "First you build the sauna, then you build the house." There are more than a million and a half saunas in Finland—about one for every four people.

Almost all apartment buildings have one or more saunas, and some companies have saunas on their premises where their employees can relax. Most of these city saunas are heated electrically instead of by a wood fire. While the results are the same, the atmosphere may not be as pleasant to the senses.

Nearly all Finns enjoy the sauna and use it regularly. They will tell you it is an excellent means of relaxation and recreation. People get together in saunas to socialize, have a bit of quiet talk, or simply meditate. Traditionally, the rural sauna, *savusauna* (SAH-voo-sow-nah), also served as a smokehouse for meat. And many women delivered their babies in a sauna— the most germ-free spot on the premises.

Nudity is the general rule in saunas. Men usually take saunas with men, and women with women. However, the family bathes together normally once a week.

Saunas are a way of life in Finland.

Land of the Midnight Sun

It never really gets dark in summer in the lands north of the Arctic Circle—but it's dark all the time in winter. Finland is one of the most northerly countries in the world; one-third of the country lies north of the Arctic Circle.

The number of hours of daylight on earth are determined by how close a place is to the North or South Pole. On the Arctic Circle there is one day of continuous sunshine called the summer solstice. At the North Pole the sun is above the horizon for six months. Time-lapse photographs taken in the far north during the summer solstice show that the sun never sets.

Auroras light up a night sky over a Finnish landscape.

DURING THE FIFTY DAYS OF WINTER WHEN THE SUN HAS moved to other climes, there is still some light from moon and stars reflecting off the snow. Occasionally the whole sky is brightened with sudden bursts of light. These celestial "fireworks"—called the aurora borealis, or the northern lights—are created when particles from the sun hit the earth's atmosphere, releasing energy in the form of light.

The shallow lakes that cover much of the center of Finland are frozen over for five or six months. Sometimes even part of the Baltic Sea freezes, making it possible to cross from Finland to Sweden on the ice. Snow covers the ground from November to April. Occasional blizzards or heavy accumulations of snow make transportation difficult and can be very destructive to the forests.

Spring is nearly unknown in Finland. By the time the ice and snow melt, in late May, wildflowers are ready to burst into bloom. Almost overnight, it is summer.

In the south, where most Finnish people live, the summer sun shines for at least twenty hours each day. Even after sun-

The midnight sun shines over the northern city of Rovaniemi.

Geographical Features

Highest Elevation:
Mount Haltia,
4,356 feet (1,328 m)

Lowest Elevation:
Sea level

Longest River: Kemi,
340 miles (547 km)

Largest Lake:
Lake Saimaa,
680 square miles (1,761 sq km)

Largest City: Helsinki

set in the southern part of Finland, twilight lingers for most of the night. The growing season is short, but the long days of sunlight and heavy summer rains help plants grow rapidly.

Autumn is especially beautiful in Finland. Brilliant yellow leaves shimmer on the birch trees, large patches of ground are covered with red berries. The sunsets are long and spectacular.

In spite of Finland's northern location, its climate is not as frigid as one might expect, thanks to a warm ocean current called the Gulf Stream. Finland's climate is similar to that of the northern United States and southern Canada. Winter temperatures seldom reach the extremes experienced in Alaska, northern Canada, and Siberia.

Finland, the seventh largest nation in Europe, is a little smaller than New Mexico and about three-fifths as big as France. The distance from south to north is 717 miles (1,154 km); from east to west at its widest, it is 336 miles (541 km).

The jagged coastline of Finland is about 682 miles (1,100 km) long. This coastline changes constantly, because the land is rising from the sea. There are tens of thousands of Finnish islands in the Baltic Sea.

Finland's borders touch Norway in the north, Russia in the east, the Baltic Sea in the south and southwest, and Sweden in the northwest. Woods and water—never far away in this country—are important elements in both work and play for most Finns.

Some of the oldest and hardest bedrock in the world underlies Finland. Geologists tell us it is 1.5 billion years old. Over millions of years, glaciers scraped away at the rocks, creating long ridges called terminal moraines. Granite outcroppings are everywhere, and soil, where it exists, is not very deep. Granite

Topographical map of Finland

Finland's lakes are full of islands.

Finnish tundra land showing dwarfed vegetation

Map of Finland's geographical districts

and limestone are quarried. Minerals in the bedrock include copper, nickel, iron, zinc, chromium, and lead. Except for copper and zinc, however, the deposits are not large enough to make mining practical.

A vast expanse of tundra lies above the Arctic Circle. (*Tundra* is a Finnish word that has become part of the English language.) It consists of a spongy mixture of soil and vegetation with a permanently frozen subsoil. There are no trees; only dwarf shrubs, lichens, and mosses grow on the tundra.

The Coastal Lowlands

Most of the Finnish people live in the Coastal Lowlands, a horseshoe-shaped region wrapped around by two arms of the Baltic Sea—the Gulf of Finland in the south and the Gulf of Bothnia in the southwest. The Coastal Lowlands are about 40 to 80 miles (65 to 130 km) wide.

This part of the country has fewer lakes and less forestland than other regions. The landscape is quite flat, with only small hills and valleys in the south. Many rivers cut through the flat, fertile land on the west, flowing to the Gulf of Bothnia. This land, the best agricultural land in Finland, has been cultivated

Farmers haying in the Oulu province in the Coastal Lowlands

for more than a thousand years. At one time much of the region was divided into large estates by the king of Sweden. Today, luxuriant orchards grow on many of these former estates.

Seafaring is an old tradition among Finns. Shipbuilding was an important industry here as early as the 1600s. The many harbors along the Gulf of Finland encouraged travel by sea. Finns also gained an early reputation for being expert navigators, steering their vessels through the obstacle courses formed by countless rocky islands.

A view from a house on the Coastal Islands

The Coastal Islands

Finland has some 180,000 islands, nearly half of them in the Baltic Sea. Many of these are just large rocks, some are skerries—rocky islets with a little vegetation—and others are large enough to hold a few summer cabins.

The Åland Islands lie in the Baltic Sea between Finland and Sweden, west of the city of Turku. Along the shores are lovely sandy beaches, spots where the forests meet the water, and natural areas frequented by large flocks of birds. About 25,000 people live on these islands, and the main language is Swedish.

The climate in the Åland Islands is milder than on the mainland, and the growing season is longer. Vegetables from the islands are shipped to the rest of the country.

The Lake District

A group of moraine ridges known as the Salpausselkä ridges (or plateau) separates the Coastal Lowlands from the large region known as the Lake District. These ridges, formed by glaciers, are sometimes called the "backbone" of Finland.

Shallow lakes, connected by streams and channels, cover one-fourth of the area. Many are so small they have no names, which makes it difficult to get a true count of the total.

Many Finns, drawn to the isolation and beauty of the Lake District, have second homes here. Transportation is

Boating in the Lake District

Church Boats

In earlier times, people in the Lake District often lived quite a distance from their nearest neighbors. The only way to get together was by boat. Churches sent boats around to gather up their parishioners on Sunday mornings, and people sang hymns as they rowed along. Frequently, the boats held impromptu races while taking families home after church. Modern versions of these "church boats" compete today in fourteen-person crew races on the lakes.

Logging on one of Finland's many lakes

possible by boat for great distances through this inland water system. On the other hand, so many bodies of water make building roads and railroads a problem. Ferries are often a necessity for connecting land routes.

There are three main groups of lakes. One drains east into the Vuoksi River and Lake Ladoga in Russia. The central system drains south down the Kymi River to the Gulf of Finland. The western group feeds the Gulf of Bothnia through the Kokemäki River.

A 35-mile (56-km) waterway, the Saimaa Canal, opened in 1856, linking Finland and Russia. The canal, used to carry goods to processing centers and to market, was part of a major transportation route until World War II began in 1939. It was closed from 1944 to 1968 but is now functioning again. Today, though many goods are carried by trucks and airplanes, inland waterways are still important, especially for the lumber industry.

In winter, the lakes are covered with solid ice and become playgrounds and roadways. People use them for skating, skiing, sledding, ice fishing, and car racing, and travel on them by ski, sleigh, and even bus.

Early settlers cleared the land in the Lake District using the "slash-and-burn" method. They cut the trees one season and burned them the next, using the ashes as fertilizer. Crops were then planted for the next few years. This farming method robbed the soil of its meager nutrients. The fields were abandoned when crops no longer flourished, and over a period of twenty to thirty years, the forests reestablished themselves. Birches grew first, followed by conifers.

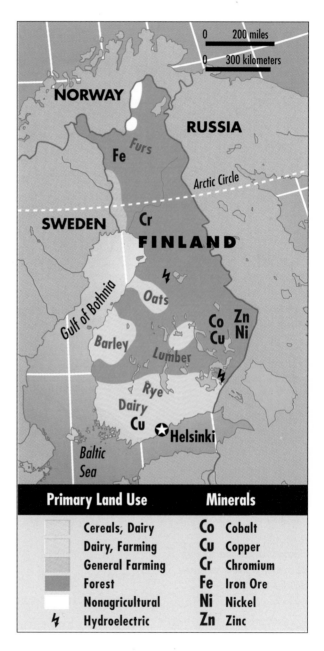

Map of Finland's natural resources

Houses in the Northland lie under a layer of snow for much of the year.

The woods and waters of the Lake District provided plenty of meat and fish for these early wilderness farmers. Today, the area has mill towns, dairy farms, small agricultural communities, and two large industrial centers—Tampere and Imatra. Both of these cities developed around sources of hydroelectric power.

Looking at Finnish Cities

Espoo is Finland's second most-populated city, followed by Tampere, Vantaa, and Turku. Each of these cities has its own special character and attractions.

Although Espoo (top) didn't receive its town charter until 1972, it was inhabited as early as 3500 B.C. Over the years, this planned garden-suburb has attracted many artists and architects. Its buildings on the Institute of Technology campus are examples of Finland's best contemporary architecture.

Tampere (middle), founded by King Gustav III of Sweden in 1779, is known for its many lakes. In fact, the city sits between two large lakes, and there almost 200 others within the city limits. Other attractions include a planetarium, a dolphinarium, and a museum devoted to the life and work of Lenin.

Located close to Helsinki, Vantaa is where the capital actually began. Today, Vantaa is best known as the home of Heureka, an excellent hands-on science center. Other attractions include the Finnish Aviation Museum and Helsinki's airport.

Turku—once the capital of Finland—dates back to the 1200s. Turku (bottom) boasts the most famous historic building in Finland—Turku Castle, founded in 1280. Much newer, but equally interesting, is the Sibelius Museum, which is dedicated to Finland's most famous composer, Jean Sibelius.

**Cross-country skiing
in Lapland**

The Northland

The northern third of Finland, above the Arctic Circle, is Lapland. Here a small wedge of low mountains extends north along the border with Sweden and Norway. The only mountains in the nation that rise more than 1,000 feet (300 m) above sea level are in the northwestern corner of this province. The highest point in Finland is the mountain of Haltia, at 4,356 feet (1,328 m). Much of the time, its summit is hidden in clouds. The rest of the region consists of high plateaus, lakes, and swamps.

Forested land extends much farther north in Finland than in Norway and Sweden, because the elevations are much lower. The few hills and mountains are bare of trees.

This Land of the Midnight Sun is a popular vacation land. The angles of light in this far northland create strange and spectacular scenes—broad vistas of snow, tundra, and glaciers. Visitors come from the south of Finland and from many other countries to camp, hike, and fish in summer and ski in winter.

Forests and Creatures

Finland stands on wooden legs—thousands and thousands of trees. Nearly three-quarters of Finland is covered with forests. It is one of the most forested nations in the world. The forests are Finland's most valuable natural resource. The country is one of the world's leading producers of wood and wood products. A little more than half of the forested land is privately owned.

Elks in a forest

Opposite: **Cloudberries and crowberries**

MOST OF THE TREES—MORE THAN 80 PERCENT—ARE conifers—evergreen trees that have needles instead of leaves. Spruce is the most common type in the south and pine in the north. The only deciduous, or leafy, tree that grows in large numbers is the birch. However, other deciduous trees are found in southern Finland, including aspens, maples, elders, elms, lindens, ashes, and oaks. Dwarfed species of birch and alder trees grow in the far north.

The rocky soil and wet climate of Finland provide ideal conditions for trees. In the central Lake District and a few other areas, forests cover as much as 80 percent of the land. Even in the southwest, where the soil is good for agriculture, forests take up 50 to 60 percent of the space.

Forest Conservation

Uninhabited land is rare in Europe. Finns guard their forest wealth carefully by gathering seeds in the forests and replanting them in nurseries.

A law was passed more than a hundred years ago to protect the forests and the habitats of wildlife. Forest rangers manage government-owned forests and supervise private forests to make sure regulations are followed. All natural elements within a forest are preserved, and features such as rocky outcroppings, bogs, streams, and marshlands must not be disturbed.

Government and landowners work out plans for preserving the forests. This science, a branch of forestry, is called *silviculture*. Forests are carefully thinned and cultivated in ways that will help to increase their growth. Finns say, "The forests will treat you the way you treat them."

Flora

Flowers and other plant life vary in Finland's forests. Thick stands of spruce trees cut off most of the sunlight from the forest floor. Pines grow in thin, rocky, and sandy soil. Birch forests offer the best environment for small plants.

There are about 1,200 species of native plants in Finland, plus 800 mosses and more than 1,000 kinds of lichens. Areas in the far north or on high mountains, where trees cannot grow because of the harsh climate, are "above the timberline." Shrubs, mosses, and lichens cover the hillsides above the timberline in Finland.

Many kinds of mushrooms are plentiful in Finland and wild berries—blueberries, lingonberries, crowberries, cloudberries, and thimbleberries—grow in large quantities. Picking these goodies on public lands is a favorite pastime for many Finns during the summer. The berries are eaten fresh or used in juices, sauces, preserves, and desserts.

Lily of the Valley

Finland's national flower is the lily of the valley, a fragrant perennial native to northern Europe, Asia, and parts of North America. A cluster of small, white, bell-shaped flowers hangs from each stem. A single plant rising from the roots has two or three broad, green leaves and several stems of flowers. The lily of the valley grows wild and is a popular plant in gardens in many parts of the world.

The elk population in Finland's forests is sizable. Here, a mother travels with twins.

Fauna

Finland's forests provide a habitat for many kinds of mammals. More than fifty species are native to the region, including wolves, foxes, and lynx, as well as smaller animals such as squirrels, lemmings, beavers, muskrats, hedgehogs, otters, and hares.

The European elk is a large deer, similar to the North American moose. These animals are a hazard on the highways so drivers need to be cautious. Bears, elks, and wolves were decreasing in numbers for a time, but they have made a comeback recently. There is now a hunting season for elk in order to keep their numbers from multiplying. Deer, introduced to Finland from North America in the 1930s, have become a threat to crops.

An otter

Wolves often cross the border into Finland from Russia. For centuries, Karelian farmers in the eastern

Bears

In a 1985 vote, the bear was chosen as Finland's national animal. Regarded as "king of the forest," the bear is the subject of many Finnish stories and legends handed down from generation to generation. Some of the songs in Finland's great national epic, the *Kalevala* (KAH-lay-vah-lah), tell these stories. They usually paint a picture of bears as gentle and dim-witted.

The bear species found in Finland is the European brown bear. Although it is somewhat smaller than Alaska's Kodiak bear, it is big enough and dangerous enough that people should keep a safe distance from it. It grows up to 6 feet (1.8 m) tall and weighs up to 500 pounds (230 kg). And though bears look clumsy, they are fast, powerful animals.

In earlier times, people were so afraid of bears that they were even superstitious about saying the word. Bear hunters were heroes, and a great celebration was held when a bear was killed.

The bear is not just feared, however, it is also respected. It is thought to have the Finnish characteristic of reliability. Today, the hunting of bears is strictly limited; only a few may be killed each year.

A dipper searches for food in icy waters.

An Arctic hare

part of the country hated wolves. Whenever one was near, they would round up a hunting group to kill it.

Animals and birds have different ways of surviving Finland's severe winters. In the Arctic, foxes and hares grow larger than in other regions and their thick fur insulates them from the cold. Arctic birds have thick plumage for the same reason. The dipper, a bird that thrives in the north, dives in icy water and swims like a seal in search of food. Small animals, such as lemmings and voles, burrow under the snow to keep warm in the winter.

Lapland is noted for its huge herds of reindeer. Wild herds once roamed the area, but today they have been replaced by domesticated herds owned by clans of Sami.

Finland has more than 300 species of birds. The larger ones include ospreys and whooper swans. Game birds such as grouse, wild ducks, and ptarmigans are also plentiful. Black

Reindeer

Some Lapps (who prefer to be called Sami) of northern Finland, Sweden, Norway, and Russia make their living by tending reindeer herds. Nearly all the Sami used to do this work, but today only a small minority do.

If you ask what part of the reindeer the Sami use, the answer is—all of it. The milk is used for drinking and dairy products, the hide is made into leather, and the meat provides food. Reindeer are also used for transportation—to pull sleds.

Reindeer eat lichen. Some lichen is found in the bark of trees and bushes, some is buried under the snow. The reindeer use their hooves to dig through the snow to find their food. The reindeer is a smaller version of the caribou, an animal found wild in the North American Arctic.

woodpeckers, ravens, and owls make their homes in wilderness areas. Bullfinches and waxwings stay all winter. Skylarks and other warblers are heard in late spring.

Migrating waterfowl and other birds gather in the peat bogs south of the tundra where 100,000 acres (40,500 ha) have been set aside as a nature preserve. People are barred from entry during most of the year.

Trout, perch, and pike swim in Finland's lakes, salmon in the rivers. Saltwater fish off the coast include cod, herring, trout, and salmon.

A flock of waxwings perches on snow-laden branches.

Swedish Rule, Russian Rule, & Independence

About 3,000 years ago, three major tribes lived in what is now southern Finland—the Finns, the Häme, and the Karelians. The tribes were subdivided into smaller groups, or clans. The people were hunters and fishers living off the bounty of the forests, the lakes, and the Baltic Sea. All their land was community property.

Another tribe, the nomadic Sami (formerly called Lapps), wandered across much of Europe north of the Arctic Circle.

FINLAND LIES BETWEEN THE SCANDINAVIAN PENINSULA AND RUSSIA. It has a long shoreline on the Baltic Sea to the south and west and many harbors. The nation's harbors and its strategic position between powerful neighbors have been both advantageous and a source of great problems for Finland.

Early on, traders from both the east and west found their way across the Baltic Sea. They traded goods such as salt and weapons for fur pelts.

Turku Castle

A tour of Turku (TOOR-koo) Castle is a walk through more than 600 years of Finnish history. The city of Turku, or Åbo (OH-boh) in Swedish, started out as a trading post on the Aura River. *Turku* is the Finnish word for "marketplace," and *Åbo* is the Swedish word for "living by the river." Turku became the center of Swedish Finland.

Karl Gustav, then governor of Finland, began building a fortress in Turku in about 1280. Towers stood at both ends; the governor's home was inside the walls. Over the next 200 years, the castle grew to more than forty rooms. There was a banquet hall, a guard room, a shooting gallery, and a suite of rooms kept ready in case the king should decide to visit. Splendid parties were held during peaceful periods.

The castle was besieged six times by various dukes seeking power over the region. Losers were thrown into prison.

In 1614, a disastrous fire destroyed everything in the castle that would burn and by 1814 the castle had fallen into ruin. Restoration was begun, but another fire in 1941 stopped work until after World War II.

Restoration was completed in 1961 and the castle is now a historical museum. Paintings, antique tapestries, and valuable pieces of furniture are on display. The Castle Church is used by the local parish; receptions and dinners are held in the banquet halls. Tourists can wander through the rooms and imagine what life might have been like here in the Middle Ages.

The Middle Ages

Christianity had spread across Europe by the eleventh century, when it split into two major groups. One group, the Roman Catholic Church, had its headquarters in Rome. The other became the Eastern Orthodox Church, based in Constantinople (now Istanbul). Rivalry between the two groups led to frequent warfare between Finland's neighbors—Roman Catholic Sweden and Eastern Orthodox Russia.

Swedish bishops were urged by the pope to send missionaries to the land of the Finns. A few Catholic priests worked in southwestern Finland to build the Church. At the same time, Eastern Orthodox missionaries were working among the Karelians, in eastern Finland.

Soon, Swedish settlers established colonies on the western and southern coasts of Finland. This was the start of a 600-year union between Sweden and Finland.

The Swedish Era

Much of Finland soon became a province of Sweden. It was called *Österland*, a Swedish word meaning "land to the east." Swedish rule over Finland was gentle for the most part. Swedish people living in Österland had some privileges not granted to Finns, but the Finns were never treated as serfs. They could vote in elections, they

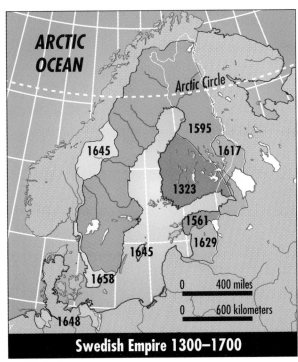

ARCTIC OCEAN

Arctic Circle

1595
1645
1617
1323
1561
1629
1645
1658
1648

0   400 miles

0   600 kilometers

Swedish Empire 1300–1700

King Gustav I Vasa

were represented in the Swedish parliament, and they had some control over local government.

In 1323, a treaty divided Karelia between Sweden and Russia. The eastern border of Finland changed many times over the next few centuries.

For a little over a hundred years, Norway, Sweden, and Denmark were united under the Danish Crown. There was quite a lot of fighting between the various factions, and the Finnish people were often the victims.

In 1523, Sweden-Finland separated from Denmark under the leadership of a nobleman who became King Gustav I Vasa. During his reign, the Protestant Reformation swept across northern Europe, and Lutheranism became the official state religion. The Finnish language then replaced Latin in church services. A Lutheran scholar, Mikael Agricola, did a great deal to encourage the use of Finnish in both writing and speech.

Decline of Swedish Power

For more than 80 of its last 300 years of rule in Finland, Sweden was at war with Denmark, Poland, or Russia. Finns were drafted to fight in these wars, and Finnish lands were often given to Swedish generals as rewards. By the mid-1600s, more than half of Finland belonged to Swedish noblemen. The Swedish people living in Finland grew more powerful, and Swedish became the language of schools and courts.

Peter the Great, czar of Russia, formed an alliance with Poland and Denmark as the 1700s began. The three countries wanted to divide up the Swedish empire among them. The Great Northern War lasted from 1700 to 1721.

The war ended with Sweden giving up some Finnish territory in the south and east. The Russians now had an outlet to the Baltic Sea, something they had long coveted. Wars over Finnish territory broke out twice more during that century. By the late 1700s the Finns were beginning to develop a sense of their own national identity and a desire to develop the land on their own terms.

The Russian Era

In 1807, Czar Alexander I of Russia and Napoleon I of France decided to divide up Europe between them. Russia invaded Finland again the next year. The czar promised the Finns that their constitutional rights and their Lutheran faith would be protected. Sweden and Russia signed a peace treaty on September 17, 1809, which created the Russian Grand Duchy of Finland. It existed for over a hundred years.

Finland was not considered a part of the Russian Empire. It was partly self-ruling under the authority of the czar, who appointed a governor general. Russia gave

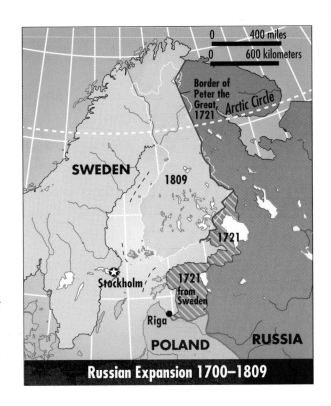

Russian Expansion 1700–1809

A woodcut of Saimaa Canal from the 1870s

back the Finnish lands they had seized during the 1700s. The Finnish laws and constitution, based on Swedish codes, were unchanged and individual rights were respected. The Russian czar simply replaced the Swedish king.

The czar moved the Finnish capital from Turku to Helsinki, which was closer to Russia's capital city, St. Petersburg. He hired planners and architects to transform Helsinki, which had suffered great devastation from fires and wartime occupations, into a first-class modern city.

Ninety years of peace in Finland followed. After all the wars, this was a welcome relief. The Saimaa Canal, which opened in 1856, was a huge improvement for the country's transportation system. Other canals were modernized, railroads were built, and roads were improved. Tar, timber, and paper could now be shipped from the interior to the ports for export abroad. Shipbuilding and the manufacture of steam engines became important industries for Finland.

Stirrings of Nationalism

First the Swedes, then the Russians, had controlled Finnish affairs for seven centuries. But the Finns remained Finns, speaking their own language, holding onto their own customs.

In 1827 a fire destroyed much of the city of Turku, including the university. Soon the institution was moved to Helsinki, where a quiet but strong Finnish nationalist movement began to grow. A slogan of the time was, "We are no longer Swedes; Russians we do not wish to become; let us be Finns."

Czar Alexander II ruled Finland with a benevolent hand. In 1863 he issued an important statement of equality—a decree that gave Finnish people equal status with Swedes. A Finnish dictionary was published, and some upper-class Swedish Finns began to study the Finnish language.

A minority of Finns were Swedish descendants. Even though their ancestors had lived in Finland for generations, they had the same fondness for the Swedish language and literature as the Finnish-

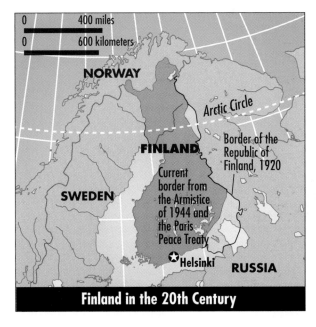

Finland in the 20th Century

speaking people had for theirs. The two groups formed their own political parties in the 1860s—the Fennomans (Finnish) and the Svecomans (Swedish).

In 1894, Czar Nicholas II came to the throne in Russia, and a harsh period, called the "Russification" of Finland, began. The czar made Russian the official language and banned free speech and free assembly. His February Manifesto of 1899 in effect put an end to Finnish self-rule. Finns reacted by launching a huge movement of passive resistance. Schoolchildren refused to learn Russian; Finnish soldiers refused to obey the orders of Russian officers.

Meanwhile, Czar Nicholas was in trouble on another front. War had broken out between Russia and Japan in February 1904. Japan won the war, and Russian revolutionary groups organized a general strike, which spread to Finland.

In 1906 the czar was pressured into allowing sweeping reforms in Finland. A Finnish one-house parliament was formed with representatives, elected by all the citizens. Women, as well as men, could vote. Finland was the first European country—and the second in the world (the first was New Zealand)—to extend full political rights to women. Suddenly, Finland was the most complete democracy in Europe.

But the Russians didn't give up. Laws were soon passed that greatly weakened Finnish self-rule, or autonomy.

In 1914 Russia entered World War I. Finland suffered economically and food shortages were widespread during the war. However, there was no fighting in Finland and very few Finns joined the military forces.

Russian rule of Finland finally ended in 1917. Revolution erupted in Russia, the czar abdicated, and Finland declared independence on December 6. By the spring of 1919, Finland had formed an independent government that was recognized by Great Britain and the United States. Soviet Russia signed a peace treaty with Finland in 1920.

Independence

There was no peace as yet, however. The years following World War I brought many hardships and challenges. Many people were out of work. There was widespread poverty and near-starvation. One out of five people in rural areas was homeless.

During the war the Finns had divided into two factions. The Red Guards, aided by Bolshevik Russia, were made up mostly of workers. Property owners and farmers formed the White Guards, who were supported by German troops. The resulting conflict brought tragic results—30,000 deaths and serious divisions in Finnish society. Both sides committed cruel acts of terrorism.

Opposite: **In 1906, women voted for the first time in Finland.**

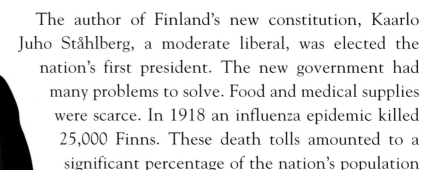

The author of Finland's new constitution, Kaarlo Juho Ståhlberg, a moderate liberal, was elected the nation's first president. The new government had many problems to solve. Food and medical supplies were scarce. In 1918 an influenza epidemic killed 25,000 Finns. These death tolls amounted to a significant percentage of the nation's population of about three million people.

The United States sent shiploads of food and a loan of ten million dollars to Finland. The country gained an excellent reputation by consistently meeting the terms of a twenty-five-year debt repayment. U.S. schoolchildren were told "Finland always pays its debts." During the twenty years following World War I, agricultural production grew rapidly. The lumber industry, along with its by-products, quickly recovered its former prominence.

Social legislation in the 1920s and 1930s provided benefits for children and safeguards in the workplace. Housing aid, insurance for accidents and disability, and old-age assistance were established. Other programs assisted mothers and young children as well as the poor, disabled, alcoholic, and mentally retarded.

The Great Depression of the 1930s affected Finland somewhat less than it did other developed European nations. Government policies bolstered the economy, which continued to grow between 1933 and 1939.

Kaarlo Juho Ståhlberg

Carl Gustaf Emil von Mannerheim

Marshal Carl von Mannerheim, a wealthy Finland-Swede who lived from 1867 to 1951, is one of Finland's great heroes. Before World War I, he served in the Russian army as commander of the czar's personal forces.

After Finland declared its independence, Mannerheim organized a Finnish army. He was appointed a temporary head of state for six months. In the years before World War II he directed the building of the Mannerheim Line, a string of fortifications in Karelia designed to keep the Soviets from invading Finland. Mannerheim led the armed forces against the Soviets during World War II. He served as president from 1944 to 1946, when he resigned because of illness.

Despite military defeats, Mannerheim is credited with helping Finland finally achieve peace with the Soviet Union.

During the Winter War of 1939–40, Finnish forces warded off the Soviets from snow-covered ditches.

Winter War

Finland's major political parties—the Social Democrats and the Agrarian Party—worked together on many social issues, making the young country more and more stable. But there was a constant fear that the Soviet Union might attack.

In August 1939 the Soviets and the Nazis signed a non-aggression pact. The Germans invaded Poland, and the Soviets seized control of Estonia, Latvia, and Lithuania. These three little countries on the Baltic Sea were Finland's close neighbors to the south.

The Soviets attacked Finland on November 30, 1939. The so-called Winter War lasted less than four months. The Finns fought fiercely, but they were no match in manpower or weapons against their giant neighbor. The Finns used antiquated cannons and rifles, as well as handmade explosives. The soldiers named these gasoline-filled bottles "Molotov

Finnish troops march east
during the Continuation War,
a conflict with the Soviet
Union during World War II.

cocktails" because many Finns blamed Russian foreign minister V. M. Molotov for starting the war.

No help came from any other nation. Soon the Finns were compelled to surrender. Peace terms were extremely harsh. Finland gave up southern Karelia, which included their second-largest city, Viipuri (now Vyborg). They also lost islands in the Gulf of Finland, a naval base at Hanko, and land in northeastern Finland. About one-eighth of the Finnish people lived on the lands taken over by the Soviet Union, and nearly all of them immediately left their homes and moved to Finnish territory.

Finland lost 25,000 troops during the Winter War; another 45,000 were wounded.

The Continuation War

In 1940, the Finns sought help from Germany to prevent another Soviet invasion. The Germans attacked the Soviets in June 1941, the Soviets launched an air attack on Finland, and on June 26 the Finns declared war on the Soviet Union.

In spite of its alliance with Germany, the Finns considered themselves to be at war only with the Soviet Union, not with the other Western Allies. They call this second conflict the Continuation War.

Finns suffered even greater losses in this second war. One out of every ten Finnish soldiers was killed, permanently disabled, or wounded. After a devastating attack on Helsinki in the spring of 1944, they were ready to talk peace terms. An armistice was signed on September 19.

The Soviets demanded that all German soldiers be expelled from Finland. Thus Finnish troops turned to fighting their former allies. The German forces retaliated by planting mines and burning forests and towns behind them as they retreated north to Norway from Finland. More than 400,000 refugees fled back into Finnish territories from the lands taken by the Soviet Union.

Postwar Challenges

Finland faced three large challenges after the war. The first was to pay the Soviet Union $300 million worth of industrial goods assessed as war reparations. The second was to help the refugees resettle and survive. The third was to achieve a good and workable relationship with Eastern Europe.

The Finns believed, as they had about their debt to the United States after World War I, that the reparation demanded by the Soviet Union was a debt of honor they had

to pay off in full. Remarkably, this debt—and the determination to pay it—had a beneficial effect on Finland's economy in the long run. Industrial development proceeded rapidly in the postwar period. Forestry, shipbuilding, and machine production flourished. A strong export business grew as the debts were paid off.

The Finnish parliament adopted the Land Act of 1945, which called for the government to purchase farmland and redistribute it to refugees and ex-servicemen. This policy enabled people who had fled Karelia, then under Soviet rule, to take part in the economic life of Finland.

Soviet influence in Eastern Europe was expanding, but the Finns were able to persuade the Soviets that strict neutrality was the best road for Finland to follow. On April 6, 1948, the two nations signed the Treaty of Friendship, Cooperation, and Mutual Assistance.

Payments to the Soviets were completed in 1952. After that, trade between the two countries increased. The Soviet Union became Finland's main trading partner, followed by Sweden, Britain, Germany, and the United States.

Representatives from Finland and the Soviet Union signed the Treaty of Friendship, Cooperation, and Mutual Assistance on April 6, 1948.

A Government of Many Parties

Finland is a truly democratic country—so democratic that Finnish elections are quite complicated. Ballots list candidates from a dozen or so political parties—another example of how much Finns value each person's right to his or her own opinion. "If you can't agree with any party, start your own," they say.

With so many parties, it is almost impossible for any one of them to win a majority of the votes. But each party has a chance to be represented in the parliament, the Eduskunta (AY-doos-koon-tah). Seats in parliament are assigned on the principle of proportional representation, so the percentage of seats given to each party equals the percentage of votes cast for that party in the election.

Posters for a variety of
candidates in Finland's 1962
presidential election

S O FAR, NO PARTY HAS EVER WON A MAJORITY OF THE SEATS. That makes it necessary for the different parties to cooperate with each other to get the work of government done.

Cooperation is as important to the Finnish way of life as independence. Finns speak of *talkoot* (TAHL-koot), a tradition of neighbors helping each other. Talkoot brought rural people together to clear fields and gather harvests, to build houses and barns, to hunt for wolves. Sometimes they pooled their money to buy farm tools together.

In 1899, Finnish dairy farmers formed a cooperative, making it possible for

Results from 1995 Parliamentary Election	
Party	Number of Seats Won
Social Democratic	63
Center Party of Finland	44
National Coalition	39
Left Wing Alliance	22
Swedish People's Party of Finland	11
Green League	9
Christian League of Finland	7
Progressive Finnish Party	2
Finnish Rural Party	1
Ecological Party	1
Other	1
Total	**200**

them to work together to get their milk and cheese to market and make sure they received fair payment. Other kinds of cooperatives, including stores and credit unions, followed. They have been an important part of the Finnish economy from their beginning.

Underlying these two traditions of independence and cooperation is a strong belief that government should help citizens enjoy a good quality of life. Legislation should be used to create a more just and humane society.

All Finnish citizens aged eighteen and over are eligible to vote, and voter turnout is normally high—averaging around 80 percent.

Chart of Finland's national government

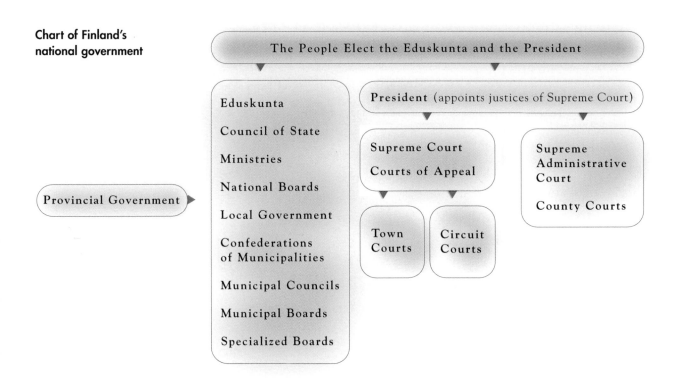

The People Elect the Eduskunta and the President

Eduskunta
Council of State
Ministries
National Boards
Local Government
Confederations of Municipalities
Municipal Councils
Municipal Boards
Specialized Boards

Provincial Government

President (appoints justices of Supreme Court)

Supreme Court
Courts of Appeal

Supreme Administrative Court
County Courts

Town Courts

Circuit Courts

During his 1994 inauguration, President Martti Ahtisaari (center) addresses the parliament. Also shown are outgoing president Mauno Koivisto (right) and speaker of the parliament Riitta Uosukainen (left).

The National Government

The Republic of Finland is governed under a constitution that went into effect on July 17, 1919. Powers are divided among three branches of government: legislative (the parliament), executive (the president and the Council of State), and judicial (the courts).

The sovereign power of Finland rests in the people through their elected parliament, Eduskunta. The 200 members of parliament are elected for four-year terms, representing fifteen electoral districts. The parliament is a one-house governmental body.

The president is the chief executive of the country. Together with the Council of State, *Valtioneuvosto* (VAHL-tee-oh-nayo-voh-sto), he or she is responsible for day-to-day operations of government. The president, who must be a native-born citizen, is elected by direct vote of the people for a term of six years.

The Council of State, made up of several political parties, is formed by the prime minister with the approval of the president. The parliament, however, can force the Council to resign and call on the president to form a new government whenever it decides such action is needed.

The prime minister and other ministers are appointed by the president, with the approval of the parliament. Currently, seventeen ministers administer twelve government bureaus:

Urho Kaleva Kekkonen

One president, Urho Kaleva Kekkonen (OOR-hoh KEHK-koh-nayn), nicknamed UKK, was president from 1956 to 1982. Before becoming president, he served as minister of justice, minister of the interior, and prime minister. Even though he was re-elected over and over, there was so much conflict among the parties that twenty-six different governments were formed during Kekkonen's time in office. Conflicts were caused by the different aims and desires of the three sectors of the economy—farm, capital, and labor.

Kekkonen, determined to bring the different factions together and establish a government of consensus, formed a popular front government in 1966. He persuaded representatives of labor and business to reach a number of agreements. Kekkonen gained widespread support and the country enjoyed prosperous times. In order to arrive at a consensus, much deal-making goes on outside the government chambers. Some critics of the consensus philosophy say that the government is simply a rubber stamp for economic decisions actually made by labor and business.

President Kekkonen retired in 1982 and died in 1986.

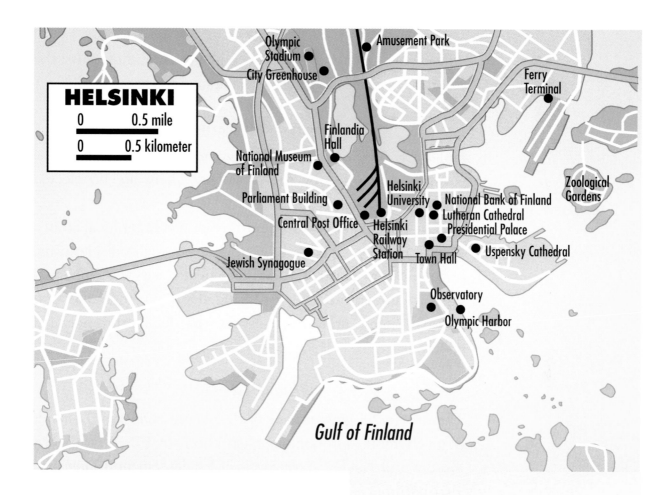

HELSINKI

0   0.5 mile

0   0.5 kilometer

Olympic Stadium

Amusement Park

City Greenhouse

Ferry Terminal

Finlandia Hall

National Museum of Finland

Zoological Gardens

Parliament Building

Helsinki University

National Bank of Finland

Central Post Office

Lutheran Cathedral

Presidential Palace

Helsinki Railway Station

Uspensky Cathedral

Jewish Synagogue

Town Hall

Observatory

Olympic Harbor

Gulf of Finland

foreign affairs, justice, interior, defense, finance, education and culture, agriculture and forestry, trade and industry, social affairs and health, communications, labor, and environment.

The courts in Finland are independent of the other branches of government. It is nearly impossible to remove judges from

Helsinki: Did You Know This?

Helsinki, founded in 1550 by decree of King Gustav I Vasa of Sweden, has been the capital city since 1812. Today, Helsinki is Finland's largest city by far and its center of commerce, industry, and the arts. Helsinki's average temperature is 63°F (17°C) in June and falls to 21°F (-6°C) in December.

office. There are three levels of courts: the Circuit Courts, the Court of Appeals, and the Supreme Court.

Provincial Government

Finland is divided into twelve provinces, each headed by a governor appointed by the president. There are no elected provincial officials.

The provincial government is responsible for local affairs. They include police work, civil defense, regional planning, price and rent control, social and health services, supervising local governments, supervising elections, and collection of taxes, fees, and revenues for the local and national government.

Åland Islands

The provincial government of the Åland (OH-lund) Islands is much more autonomous than those of other provinces. Most island residents are Swedish by descent and language. Two national acts with constitutional status guarantee the preservation of Swedish traditions and way of life on the islands.

Local Government

The tradition of local self-government dates from the early days of Christianity in Finland. Until the 1800s the Church was the major local authority. Today the communities are responsible for education and health matters.

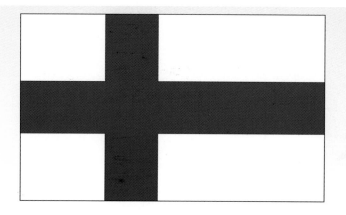

The Flag

The Finnish flag, used since the nation's independence, is a light-blue cross on a white field. The cross is horizontal, with the intersection of the two legs to the left of center. The colors of the flag symbolize the colors of nature in Finland. The blue represents the blue of the thousands of lakes; the white is for the pure winter snows.

Municipal councils are elected for four-year terms, and seats are assigned by proportional representation. The routine work is carried out by a municipal board of seven or more members. They are selected from the councils and serve two-year terms.

Participation in government at the local level is widespread, and most politicians begin their careers as council members.

Foreign Policy

Finland's location and history have taught the Finns an important lesson: the country must get along with its neighbors if it is to survive. During the Cold War, for example, Finland's leaders avoided capture by either the Eastern or Western bloc by staying friendly with both the United States and the Soviet Union. Finland's friendship with the Soviet Union was always a wary one, but it worked to great economic

Finland's Presidents	
K. J. Ståhlberg	1919–25
L. K. Relander	1925–31
P. E. Svinhufvud	1931–37
Kyösti Kallio	1937–40
Risto Ryti	1940–44
C. G. E. Mannerheim	1944–46
J. K. Paaskivi	1946–56
U. K. Kekkonen	1956–82
Mauno Koivisto	1982–94
Martti Ahtisaari	1994–

Finland's delegation attends the fifty-first session of the UN's General Assembly in 1996.

benefit for both nations. At the same time, the nation had strong ties with the West. Finland was the only country in Europe that maintained solid trade relations with both East and West Germany without official diplomatic recognition.

Finland has been a solid supporter of the United Nations and its objectives. It became a UN member in 1955, has been an elected member of the UN Security Council twice, and is a frequent member of the Economic and Social Council and other UN agencies.

The foreign trade policy of Finland is aimed at protecting its own interests and working toward international elimination of trade barriers. Disarmament has also been a major foreign policy objective. The country has been active in promoting the limitation and control of nuclear weapons. In 1969, Helsinki hosted the first Strategic Arms Limitation Talks (SALT) between the United States and the Soviet Union.

The most important foreign policy event in Finland's history to date took place in 1975. The heads of thirty-five nations, including President Gerald Ford of the United States, met in Helsinki to sign the European security agreement called the Helsinki Accord.

In 1975, leaders of thirty-five nations met in Finland's capital to sign the Helsinki Accord.

"Our Land"
The Finnish National Anthem

Our land, our land, our native land,
Oh let her name ring clear!
No peaks against the heav'ns that stand,
No gentle dales or foaming strand
Are loved as we our home revere,
The earth our sires held dear.

The flowers in their buds that grope
Shall burst their sheaths with spring;
So from our love to bloom shall ope
Thy gleam, thy glow, thy joy, thy hope,
And higher yet some day shall ring
The patriot song we sing!

By: *Johan Ludvig Runeberg*
Translation by: *Charles Sharton Stork*

Environmental Protection

The importance of international cooperation to protect the environment was made alarmingly clear in 1986. Fallout from a nuclear calamity at the Chernobyl power plant in Soviet Ukraine had a disastrous effect in Finnish Lapland. Hundreds of reindeer had to be killed.

Environmental issues rank high on Finnish voters' priority lists. Several minor political parties run on a "green" platform, and major parties also recognize the importance of environmental concerns. The basic issues are the same as those in the rest of the world. Air and water pollution, destruction of natural areas, overconsumption of energy, and waste management are among the problems to be faced.

Agricultural practices such as clearing forests, draining wetlands, fertilizer runoff, and overusing soil threaten the purity of the lake waters. Manufacturing plants emit harmful substances into the air. Russia, Poland, and Germany have all added to the pollution of the Baltic Sea.

In comparison to other European countries, though, Finland appears to be in much better shape.

The Wilderness Act of 1991 set aside twelve areas in Lapland to be kept in their natural state. There are no roads into these preserves, and tree cutting is strictly controlled. Finnish industries are working on the problems along with the state. Researchers and designers are seeking cleaner methods of processing materials and innovative ways to reuse them.

The Nordic Council

The Nordic Council, an international advisory body, was established in the mid-1950s. The council makes it possible for member democracies—Finland, Sweden, Norway, Denmark, and Iceland—to function in many ways like a single large nation.

Citizens of all five countries can move freely throughout the region without visas or passports. They do not need work permits to work in another Nordic nation. If they establish residence for two years in a sister nation they can vote in that country's elections. They are entitled to the same health care and other social benefits as native-born citizens.

The presidents and other leaders of the five member countries meet face-to-face once a year and discuss solutions to common problems. The Sami are also represented but have no vote.

Cooperation across borders touches many aspects of life. Many laws and regulations are similar throughout the region. Environmental protection, education, scientific research, industry, and energy are among the subjects of concern to the council.

In 1995, Finland became
the fifteenth nation to
join the European Union
(EU), formerly known as
the European Community.
This organization works
for agreement among the
members on matters
affecting trade and free
movement of people
across the borders of
member states. It also
works to promote the eco-
nomic advancement of
poorer regions.

European Union leaders
pose for a "family portrait"
at a 1996 conference.

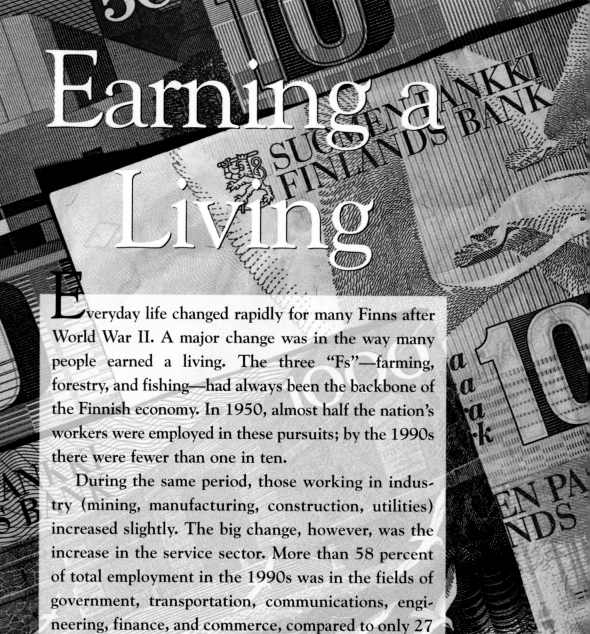

Earning a Living

Everyday life changed rapidly for many Finns after World War II. A major change was in the way many people earned a living. The three "Fs"—farming, forestry, and fishing—had always been the backbone of the Finnish economy. In 1950, almost half the nation's workers were employed in these pursuits; by the 1990s there were fewer than one in ten.

During the same period, those working in industry (mining, manufacturing, construction, utilities) increased slightly. The big change, however, was the increase in the service sector. More than 58 percent of total employment in the 1990s was in the fields of government, transportation, communications, engineering, finance, and commerce, compared to only 27 percent in 1950.

FINLAND'S GOVERNMENT PLAYS AN IMPORTANT PART IN sponsoring economic development. For example, it protects domestic agriculture. The aim is to preserve the family farm in order to keep the nation fairly self-sufficient in food production. On the other hand, government has generally not stepped in to bail out declining industries.

Once the payment of war reparations was finished, Finland's gross national product grew steadily—and faster than the average of other industrialized countries. A strong social welfare system spread the wealth among all sectors of society. The two biggest changes in Finland's economy, like those of many other countries of the industrialized world, are the increased numbers of international corporations and the rapid increase in high-tech industries.

The worldwide oil crises of 1973 and 1979 were hard on Finland, because four-fifths of the nation's primary energy supplies were imported. The government introduced an austerity

Although Finns are increasingly likely to work in service-related industries, fishers still sell their catch at harbor markets.

program in 1978 to help keep Finnish industry competitive in the world. By the 1980s, in spite of the slowdown, Finland was one of the most prosperous countries in the world and enjoyed one of the highest standards of living.

A more serious blow to Finnish economy came with the collapse of trade agreements with Russia in the early 1990s. Finland and Russia had long practiced a barter system in exports: Finnish heavy machinery in return for oil. When Russia could no longer keep its end of the bargain, many Finns lost their jobs. Unemployment was Finland's major problem in the 1990s. By 1994 Russia had fallen from first to fifth place in the list of Finland's export markets.

Most of Finland's industrial plants are located in the southern part of the country. Almost all the big companies are based in Helsinki.

Forest Products

Although fewer people work in forestry today, trees are still Finland's greatest natural resource. Many other industries are related to wood, either directly or indirectly. Finnish companies convert lumber into wood and paper products. Forest products include pulp, paper, paperboard, plywood, and particle board. Finland ranks second in the world, after Canada, in paper exports.

Finnish factories also manufacture timber-harvesting equipment and machinery for making paper and related products. Finnish experts design machinery for manufacturers throughout the world.

Opposite: **Forest products are a mainstay of Finland's economy. This factory produces wood pulp.**

What Finland Grows, Makes, and Mines

Agriculture

Barley	1,764 metric tons
Sugar beets	1,110 metric tons
Oats	1,097 metric tons

Manufacturing

	Percent of all manufacturing output
Food products	17
Paper and paper products	16
Machinery (especially for papermaking)	9

Mining*

Gold

Zinc ore

Silver

* Mining accounts for a statistically minor amount of the total agricultural and industrial output in Finland. Both mineral deposits and mineral yields are very small.

Prefabricated wooden buildings are produced in Finland. Japan and European countries buy houses, cottages, and saunas, as well as ready-made schools, hospitals, factories, and other public buildings.

Other Manufacturing

Nearly 40 percent of Finland's exports come from the metal and engineering industry. Finnish companies are active in research, development, and the use of modern automation and industrial robots.

Generators, transformers, and motors are made in Finland for use in icebreakers and locomotives. The electrotechnical industry also includes the manufacture of batteries, bulbs, telephones,

TV sets, medical electronics, and communications systems. This industry has been one of the fastest growing in recent years.

Finns have been shipbuilders for centuries. Today, they concentrate on specialties such as icebreakers, cruise ships, barges, oil-drilling rigs and drill ships, and smaller boats for pleasure and work. Boatbuilders turn out about 31,000 boats a year, including more than 5,000 for export. Other transportation products include automobiles, bicycles, mopeds, trams, heavy-duty trucks, and railway locomotives.

The chemical industry is fairly new in Finland, but it has become very important to the national economy. More than 200 companies, many of them quite small, manufacture chemicals. Products include basic chemicals, fertilizers and pesticides, drugs and medicines, paints and inks, plastics, detergents, cosmetics, and toiletries.

About 600 factories in Finland manufacture textiles and clothing. More than half of these goods are sold at home, but exports have been increasing for a number of years. Knitwear, outdoor sports-

Finnish textile companies, such as Marimekko, the well-known fabric producer, export their goods around the world.

wear, and fur and leather goods are among the more important products. Finland is one of the largest exporters of farmed furs in the world, and some sixty companies manufacture leather footwear, with a concentration on winter shoes and boots. Nearly half the total production is exported.

Food-processing in Finland is extensively automated. About 85 percent of the food consumed domestically is produced from local raw materials. Food and beverage exports include cheese, chocolates, infant formulas, butter, and a few specialties. These specialties, well known around the world, include rye rusks and crispbread, vodka, and liqueurs made from local berries.

Service Industries

Merchant shipping, ferrying passengers in the Baltic Sea, design consulting, and tourism are among the activities that have helped the service sector of the economy increase more rapidly than manufacturing in recent years.

Finland was discovered as a desirable vacation spot by the aristocracy and wealthy class of St. Petersburg, Russia, more than a century ago. Swedes, Estonians, and Britons started traveling to Finland in the 1920s and 1930s. In 1952, the Summer Olympics held in Helsinki showed the world what Finland has to offer visitors.

Tourism accounts for about 1 percent of Finland's gross national product and gives jobs to more than 70,000 full-time employees and many seasonal workers. Publishing and printing of newspapers, periodicals, and books employs about 38,000 workers.

Design

Finland has a worldwide reputation in the field of modern design. Graduates of Finland's University of Industrial Design create shapes and forms for such products as telephones, computers, machinery, and many other items used in daily life. One example familiar around the world is a particular type of scissors with orange handles.

Finnish designers are often called on to consult for industries in other countries.

Family Economics

The average annual income per worker in Finland in 1994 was 81,717 FIM, or about $18,000. About half of household expenditures went for food and housing. Transportation and communication

Well-known scissors of Finnish design

Finnish Currency

Finnish money is based on the *markka* (MAHRK-kah), usually referred to outside the country as the Finnmark (FIM). Bills are in denominations of 10, 20, 50, 100, 500, and 1,000 marks. They carry pictures of famous Finns.

The 10-FIM bill features athlete Paavo Nurmi on the front and Helsinki's Olympic Stadium on the back. The new 20-FIM bill pictures Väinö Linna, author of the best-selling novel *The Unknown Soldier*. The portrait on the 50 is architect Alvar Aalto, with Finlandia Hall, which he designed, on the reverse. The face on the 100 is of composer Jean Sibelius. The 500-FIM bill features Elias Lönnrot, author of the epic poem, the *Kalevala*; the 1,000 has a picture of Anders Chydenius, an eighteenth-century religious leader and economist.

The markka equals 100 pennis. Coins come in 10 and 50 pennis, as well as 1, 5, and 10 markkas. Coins are decorated with plants, birds, mammals, and stars. The 5-markka piece has a symbolic Lake Saimaa Ringed Seal (Norppa).

took another 19 percent, clothing about 5 percent, health and medical care, 3.5 percent.

The standard of living of most Finnish families, in terms of material possessions, is relatively high. On average, more than nine out of ten households have a color TV, seven have a car, six have videocassette recorders, and more than three have either compact disc players or computers, or both. Refrigerators, freezers, microwave ovens, dishwashers, and telephones are standard equipment in most homes in Finland.

Mobile telephones are more common than in North America on a per capita basis. The sound of a ringing phone can be heard on buses or trains, on the streets—almost anywhere in a Finnish city.

Ihmiset— The People

Only a little more than five million people live in Finland. More than 98 percent of them were born in Finland and share a common ancestry. Not many other countries in the world have such a homogeneous, or similar, population.

Finland is one of the smallest countries in Europe in population. In land area, however, it is the seventh largest. Since most of the people live in the southern part of the country, there are many open spaces in the north.

Are the Finns Scandinavians?

SCANDINAVIA, A SOMEWHAT INEXACT TERM, HAS BEEN USED for centuries to refer to certain parts of northern Europe. Geographically, it usually means the Scandinavian Peninsula (Norway and Sweden) and Denmark.

Culturally, however, the two countries of Iceland and Finland have much in common with the other three and the history of the five nations has been closely intertwined for the last thousand years. Therefore it is considered correct to refer to the five nations—Denmark, Finland, Iceland, Norway, and Sweden—as Scandinavia. The word "Nordic" also refers to the five Scandinavian nations.

Language

Until the late 1800s, Swedish was the language of business, government, and education in Finland. Then the rise of the Finnish nationalist movement resulted in the use of written Finnish in schools and the emergence of a well-educated Finnish-speaking class.

Independence and a new constitution gave equal status to both Swedish and Finnish. Today, either language can be

Map of the population distribution in Finland

Persons per sq. mi.	Persons per sq. km.
25-125	10-50
2-25	1-10
fewer than 2	fewer than 1

Pronunciation Key

The strong stress, or accent, in all Finnish words is on the first syllable of the word. Long words may have a secondary stress, but the emphasis is always on the first syllable. Here are some clues for pronouncing letters that might be confusing.

Consonants

h	always pronounced, never silent
ng	pronounced g as in singer not hard g as in finger
r	always rolled
j	pronounced y as in yellow
s	pronounced s as in so

Vowels

ä	pronounced a as in cat
ö	pronounced er as in number

Common Finnish Words and Phrases

Hello	*Hei* or *Terve* (HIGH or TAYR-vay)
Good-bye	*Näkemiin* (NAH-ke-meen)
Thank you	*Kiitos* (KEE-tohs)
What is your name?	*Mikä sinun nimi on?* (MIK-ah SI-noon NIMI OAN)
Where are you from?	*Mistä olet kotoisin?* (MISS-tah OAL-et KOA-toy-sin)
How are you?	*Mitä kuuluu?* (MI-tae KOO-loo)
I'm fine, thanks.	*Kiitos hyvää.* (KEE-tohs HEW-vae)

In parts of Finland, signs display information in Finnish and Swedish. These road signs are on the freeway between Tampere and Helsinki.

used in court proceedings and official documents. State radio and television broadcasts are given in both languages; all national laws are issued in both.

The Finnish language is unlike most other languages. It is related to Estonian, Hungarian, Lapp, and a few other languages in the Finno-Ugric family, but it has no similarity to the languages of other Scandinavian countries.

In some ways Finnish is easy to learn because it has no articles or genders. It is completely phonetic with no silent letters, so words are easy to spell. On the other hand, nouns have as many as fifteen different endings, signifying different cases. Virtually all verbs have 128 different conjugations and personal forms.

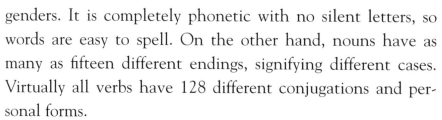

About 6 percent of Finland's population speak Swedish as their first language. They are descended mostly from the Swedish settlers and the elite who once governed Finland, and their people have been here for a thousand years. Most of them live along the western and southern coasts and in the Åland Islands.

Schools in Finland today require students to know at least two languages. Some adults speak as many as half a dozen lan-

guages. All Swedish-speaking children start learning Finnish in the third grade. Finnish-speaking pupils start English in the third grade, and usually begin to learn Swedish in the seventh. There is a great deal of intermarriage between the Swedish- and Finnish-speaking people.

"My mouth is Swedish, but my heart is Finnish," is a saying that illustrates the patriotism Swedish-speaking Finns feel for their country.

A busy outdoor market in Helsinki, Finland's most-populated city

Where They Live

Until World War II ended, most Finns were rural people. Farms and forests provided their livelihood. Nomadic Sami in the far north earned their living by raising large herds of reindeer.

Five Largest Towns in Finland (1995)

Helsinki	525,031
Espoo	191,247
Tampere	182,742
Vantaa	166,480
Turku	164,744

The Sami

You have probably heard of Lapland, but there is no such nation. The Sami, or Lapps as they used to be called, are a distinct ethnic group who lived in the north of Europe long before the Finns arrived. More than 40,000 Sami live north of the Arctic Circle in Norway, Sweden, and part of Russia, including about 4,000 in Finland.

Reindeer-herding was the primary occupation of the Sami until recent years. Now most Sami live in permanent houses, wear European clothing, and work at a variety of jobs. Visitors only occasionally see herders dressed in traditional colorful costumes.

The Sami tradition was deeply rooted in living close to nature. Only a generation or two ago, a young Sami was taught that all he needed to survive in the wilderness was a sharp knife.

The landscape of Lapland has seen many changes since World War II. New communities have sprung up and new roads have been built. Rivers have been tamed to create two new man-made lakes and produce hydroelectric power. Tourists from the south of Finland and from other countries have discovered the pleasures of hiking in Lapland, through some of the last unspoiled stretches of wilderness in Europe.

The Sami are represented in the Nordic Council, along with the leaders of the five member nations. They have a voice in deliberations but no vote. They have their own publication, theater, and arts and crafts organizations. Today, they are struggling to maintain their own language and culture as the outside world creeps into their lands.

In 1940 and 1944 part of the region in southeastern Finland known as Karelia was ceded to the Soviet Union. Most Finns living there chose to resettle in other parts of rural Finland. This resettlement increased the number of farms in the country for a short time.

In the 1960s and 1970s many Finnish farmers left rural areas in search of work. Jobs in agriculture and forestry were decreasing in number and people were drawn to the cities of the south by opportunities in white-collar and service industries.

Today about 60 percent of all Finnish people live in towns and cities. Nearly one out of every three lives in one of the country's ten largest towns, and one out of five lives in the greater Helsinki area.

Movement and Growth of Population

Finland is among the slowest of modern nations in population growth for two reasons—a comparatively low birth rate and migration. About three million people lived in the country before World War I. In 1992, the number exceeded five million.

Residents of Sweden and Finland have moved back and forth between the two countries for centuries. The first Swedes settled in Finland in the Middle Ages; Finns began emigrating to Sweden in the 1500s. Many Finns also emigrated to North America. Between the mid-1800s and late 1900s, about 400,000 Finnish people settled in the United States and Canada.

The number of foreign-born people living in Finland has grown considerably in recent years. There were four times as many in 1995 as in 1985. However, the foreign-born population is still a small minority—only about 1.3 percent of the overall population. Some are refugees from Russia and from African and Asian countries.

A Romany merchant sells her handiwork.

The few small minority groups who have lived here for generations differ from the majority more by language or religion than by ties to other lands. They include about 4,400 Sami in the north; 5,000 to 6,000 Romanies (formerly known as Gypsies) scattered throughout Finland; and a few hundred Jews and Muslims who live mostly in Turku and Helsinki.

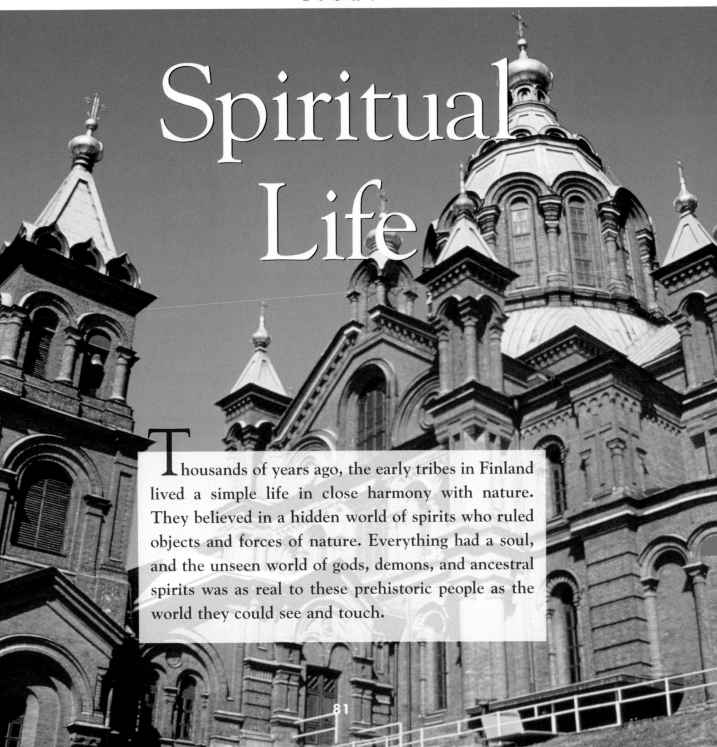

Spiritual Life

Thousands of years ago, the early tribes in Finland lived a simple life in close harmony with nature. They believed in a hidden world of spirits who ruled objects and forces of nature. Everything had a soul, and the unseen world of gods, demons, and ancestral spirits was as real to these prehistoric people as the world they could see and touch.

THE MOST POWERFUL GOD WAS *UKKO*, GOD OF THUNDER AND lightning. (The Finnish word for thunder is *ukkonen*, pronounced OOK-koa-nayn.) *Ilmarinen* was a superhuman blacksmith who created the heavens. He gave fire to humans and taught people how to use it to fashion iron objects. *Tapio* and his wife *Tellervo* were god and goddess of the woods. Hunters trusted *Tapio* to lead them to their prey and sacrificed the first kill to him.

Vellamo was the goddess of the water. *Pellervoinen* was god of the fields, especially of corn and barley. *Egres* was the god of vegetation and fertility. Another vegetation god was *Sampsa*, who slept all winter. Spring, and a new growing season, began when he awakened.

Certain priests, or shamans, were thought to have special powers to influence natural events. They interpreted the spirit world to the community. They could cure the sick and persuade some of the hidden spirits not to do harm.

The worship of many gods disappeared slowly as Christianity became nearly universal in Finland. But the love of the land, the forests, the water, and the belief in staying close to nature continue to be important traits in the Finnish national character.

Christianity

Roman Catholic missionaries came into southwest Finland from Sweden during the Middle Ages. They converted nearly all of the inhabitants to that faith. At the same time, Finnish people in the southeast—Karelians—were recruited into the Eastern Orthodox Church.

Catholic monks and priests built a convent and church in southwest Finland in the 1400s. The town of Naantali grew

Opposite: **Turku's cathedral dates back to the early 1200s.**

Mikael Agricola, Bishop of Turku

A young student in southwestern Finland was working as a scribe and assistant to Martti Skytte, the bishop of Turku, in the 1530s. Mikael Agricola and his employer were interested in the new ideas and ideals preached by Martin Luther, father of the Reformation. The Swedish Church had broken official ties with Rome and the pope. Bishop Skytte felt the church would be much more effective if it used the language of the people instead of Latin. He started holding church services in both Swedish and Finnish.

Following the bishop's example, Mikael started to translate the Bible into Finnish. The bishop was impressed with Mikael's work, and he sent him to Wittenberg, Germany, to continue his studies under Luther.

Mikael returned in 1539 with personal letters of recommendation from Luther. He served for a while as a schoolmaster. He created the first Finnish-language primer, printed in 1543, to help the people learn to read in their own language. The book also contained a catechism—a series of questions and answers about religious doctrine.

Mikael Agricola was appointed bishop of southwestern Finland, the highest office in the Finnish church, in 1554. He did not live long enough to translate the entire Bible, but he did publish a New Testament, parts of the Old Testament, a prayer book, and other religious works. A motto in the prayer book said that surely God could understand prayers offered in Finnish.

Agricola's were the first books published in the Finnish language. For this reason he is known as the father of Finnish literature. Two important results came from these efforts: literacy was greatly increased, and in 1640, Åbo Academy was established. The Academy was moved to Helsinki in 1832, and its name was changed to the University of Helsinki. (In 1919, a private Swedish-speaking university named Åbo Akademi was founded in Turku.)

up around them. The church, restored in the 1960s, has a fine
organ. Famous organists travel long distances to enjoy playing
this instrument. Each June a music festival draws some 15,000
visitors to the tiny seaside resort.

A Lutheran church service
in today's Finland

The Convent Church is now Lutheran, but one tradition
of the Catholic days is carried on. On summer evenings, ves-
per trumpet concerts are played from the tower.

When the German monk Martin Luther started the Protestant
Reformation, a number of Finnish scholars were influenced by his

ideas. Lutheranism gradually replaced Catholicism. In the 1500s, Lutheran was proclaimed the state religion.

The church took most of the responsibility for education before and during the Reformation. In 1686 a church law required people to prove they could read before they were allowed to marry.

Today, a large majority of the population belongs to the Evangelical-Lutheran Church of Finland. There are a number of revivalist and evangelical groups within the Lutheran Church.

The Orthodox Church of Finland is also recognized as an official church. When Finland was part of Russia, services in the Orthodox Church began to be conducted in Finnish. It severed ties with the Russian Orthodox Church and connected once again with the ecumenical patriarch in Constantinople.

Members of the Orthodox Church make up a small portion of the population, but the church has seen a modest growth among young people in recent years. A few Orthodox chapels are scattered throughout the country where Karelians have resettled since leaving Soviet Karelia.

While many Finnish people are not churchgoers, most of them are baptized, confirmed, married, and buried with church rites. The church traditions seem important at these key moments in life.

Freedom of religion is guaranteed in present-day Finland by the Constitution of 1919 and the Freedom of Religion Act.

Churches in Helsinki

Three churches in Helsinki represent different faiths, different periods, and strikingly different architecture.

The oldest is the Lutheran Cathedral (top), one of three splendid neoclassic buildings that front on Senate Square. The cornerstone was laid in 1832. The other two structures are the Council of State and the main building of Helsinki University. All of them were designed by renowned German architect Carl Ludvig Engel as part of the czar's plan to turn Helsinki into a world-class city with broad streets, open squares, and superb architecture.

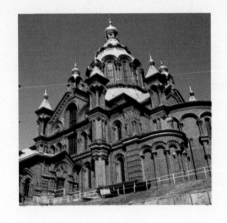

Uspensky Cathedral (middle), the largest Orthodox church in Scandinavia, is a Byzantine-Slavic building of red brick with four granite supporting pillars and a central cupola. This house of worship was completed in 1868 and restored a hundred years later. Its decidedly Russian appearance has made it the choice of some filmmakers as a backdrop for a scene that is supposedly taking place in Moscow.

Temppeliaukio Church (bottom), consecrated in 1969, is a unique, thoroughly modern building. It was built into a granite quarry, with unfinished natural stone forming the walls of the church. The sanctuary is below street level. A skylit dome made of copper wire is surrounded by a low wall of stone from the quarry.

Finlandia, the Moomins, and Olympic Gold

Twice a year the face of Finland changes abruptly. In summer it is green and blue, the colors of trees and lakes. In winter it is white with snow and ice. The land, the weather, and the seasons influence everything that is Finnish. Writers, artists, musicians, and designers draw their inspiration from nature. The changing seasons are marked with special holidays.

A Midsummer celebration

Mᴀʏ ꜰɪʀsᴛ ɪs Mᴀʏ Dᴀʏ ᴏʀ *Vᴀᴘᴘᴜ* (VAHP-poo), a celebration of the coming of summer. On this day, it is traditional for people to wear the white caps they received when they graduated from secondary school. Since graduation is traditionally held on the last day of May, new graduates have to wait eleven months for Vappu and the chance to wear their school caps. People of all ages come out on the streets to greet friends and neighbors, and white caps are ceremoniously placed on statues.

Midsummer or *Juhannus* (YOOH-hahn-noos) is the nation's biggest holiday, celebrated on Friday night and Saturday between June 20 and 26. It is the longest day of the year and also the Finnish Flag Day. Everyone takes part— swimming, boating, and consuming lots of holiday food and drink. Bonfires are built in nearly every town or community, usually on a shore or on an offshore island. Huge piles of wood, often including old boats, are set ablaze.

Weddings

Fall was once the favorite time of year for weddings, when the harvest was in. Today's Finns, however, prefer Midsummer. More weddings are performed during this holiday than at any other time of year. At each bonfire, a wedding couple is given the honor of setting the wood ablaze.

Folk traditions associate this celebration with growth and fertility. On Midsummer nights, unmarried girls tie nine herbs into a tiny bouquet and sleep with it under their pillow, hoping to dream of their future bridegroom.

Handicraft traditions were associated with weddings. Young girls would fill a decorated trunk with handmade textiles, linens, and dresses. Young men, especially in western Finland, made a variety of carved wooden objects to give to their brides. These customs are not as common as they once were, but folk handicraft is becoming popular again.

Venetian Night, in late August, celebrates the end of the summer season on the west coast with fireworks, concerts, and bonfires. Some communities hold arts and crafts fairs at this time of year.

In the city of Tampere, the long winter nights are brightened from October to January—the Weeks of Light. Thousands of tiny white lights and many decorations are displayed—not just Christmas figures but fairies and storybook creatures as well.

Christmas is celebrated with great enthusiasm in Finland. Some Finns will inform you, quite convincingly, that Santa Claus and his reindeer live in northern Finland. Finland's national airline, Finnair, carries the slogan "The Official Airline of Santa Claus." But tradition says that Santa comes by sled to deliver presents to Finnish children on Christmas Eve.

Holidays in Finland

New Year's Day	(January 1)
Epiphany	(January 6)
Good Friday	
Easter	
May Day Eve and Day	(April 30 and May 1)
Ascension Day	
Whitsun	
Midsummer Eve and Day	(coincides with the summer solstice)
Independence Day	(December 6)
Christmas Eve and Day	(December 24 and 25)
Boxing Day	(December 26)

Literature

In 1802 a Finnish infant was born who would grow up to have a great influence on Finnish literature, as well as on the future history of the country. Elias Lönnrot's family was poor, but he got a good education and became a country doctor. His main interest, though, was in the folk songs and stories of his people.

Elias made many trips into small villages on foot or skis. He was looking for "rune singers," or folk singers, who knew and performed traditional poems and songs. Elias listened carefully and wrote down everything he heard. He was encouraged by the Finnish Literature Society, which helped finance his travels and published his first work.

The doctor's collection grew and grew. He edited the songs and wove the themes, characters, and plots together into an epic poem, the *Kalevala*. Lönnrot was thirty-three when his famous work was published. It was the first truly Finnish literature. His second book was a collection of lyric folk poems called the *Kanteletar*, "Daughter of the Kantele." (The kantele is a stringed instrument often used to accompany folk singing.)

The young doctor was intensely interested in preserving and promoting the unique folk heritage of his people. His influence went far beyond his expectations. The *Kalevala* became the foundation of literature in the Finnish language. Its stories of people facing hostile and nonhuman powers, sometimes overcoming them through magic, were interpreted as symbolic of the struggles of the Finns themselves.

The Finns had no written language until the 1500s, when Mikael Agricola constructed an alphabet and translated parts of the Bible into Finnish. His work was followed by the publication of a few religious and educational works in Finnish. However, until the *Kalevala*, fiction was exclusively in Swedish. The *Kalevala* introduced the culture and traditions of Finland to the world. It has been translated into more than

Opposite: **Johan Ludvig Runeberg (1804–77) is considered Finland's greatest poet.**

thirty languages, including five translations into English.

Several other Finnish authors published books during the nineteenth century. Johan Ludvig Runeberg wrote *Tales of the Ensign Ståhl*, in Swedish. It includes the poem "Our Land," which became the words to the Finnish national anthem. Zacharias Topelius wrote fairy tales and textbooks, also in Swedish. Minna Canth was the first major Finnish-language playwright; her works are still performed today.

An epic novel by Aleksis Kivi, *Seven Brothers*, is regarded as one of the most important works in all Finnish literature. The story deals with men who wanted to live simply, off the land. They resisted efforts of the village leaders to educate and civilize them. Incidentally, the Finnish word *sivistys* (SI-viss-tewss) means both "education" and "civilization" in English. Literary scholars compare the brothers' efforts to stay free of the demands of polite society with *The Adventures of Huckleberry Finn* by Mark Twain. Kivi also wrote plays, including the first comedy and the first tragedy in

The Moomins

Finland's most beloved children's stories are the work of an artist and author named Tove Jansson. She has written and illustrated dozens of books. Favorites are the Moomin stories and picture books, which have been translated into more than thirty languages.

The Moomins have found their way into cartoon strips and a television series. Moomin characters have also performed on stage, in operas, in films and videos, and on radio.

The major Moomin characters are Moominpappa, Moominmamma, and their son, Moomintroll. They all live together in Moominhouse, a blue, towerlike home in Moominvalley. The stories are full of action and adventure, with the good characters always coming out on top.

Original illustrations and figures of Moomin characters are on display in the Tampere Public Library, in a special section called Moominvalley. There is a multivisual show and an interactive computerized Moominhouse.

Moomin World is a theme park on Kailo, a wooded island offshore from Naantali, on Finland's west coast. Opened in 1993, it is quite different from some of the world's larger and fancier theme parks. There are no rides and no souvenirs for sale in Moomin World. Children can walk through Moominhouse and Moominpappa's boat, touch and play with objects, take part in Moomin performances, and run and play all over the island.

Jansson's Moomin books have a lighthearted touch of fantasy. The stories involve adventures that might remind readers a little of *Alice in Wonderland* and *Winnie the Pooh*. In fact, Jansson has also contributed illustrations for books by Lewis Carroll and A. A. Milne.

Tove Jansson has won countless international awards for her books and illustrations since the first Moomin book was published in 1945.

Finnish. Indeed, Kivi's own life was tragic. He died in a mental asylum at the age of thirty-eight.

Literature in both Finnish and Swedish has flourished in the 1900s. Themes often deal with relationships of humans with nature, with one another, and with society. Frans Eemil Sillanpää won the Nobel Prize for Literature in 1939. His major works are *Meek Heritage* and *The Maid Silja*. One of the best-known and most widely read Finnish novels is *The Unknown Soldier* by Väinö Linna, published in 1954.

The government helps support writers in Finland through numerous grants and prizes. More books are published in this country per capita than in any other. Finnish people are great readers. They buy books and borrow them from libraries in large numbers. There are 1,500 public libraries, and a fleet of bookmobiles travels to more than 18,000 locations. Videos and records can be borrowed as well as books.

Music and Dance

Music is everywhere in Finland. Most towns have community orchestras and choral societies. International music festivals are hosted in major cities each year, and concert tickets are always sold out far in advance. In addition, hundreds of smaller communities throughout the country present folk, symphonic, opera, jazz, rock, religious, and other types of music.

The nation's greatest and best-known composer is Jean Sibelius, born in 1865. He composed seven symphonies and a number of shorter works. Sibelius became internationally

famous at the Paris Exhibition in 1900, when the Helsinki City Orchestra played some of his compositions. One piece in particular, *Finlandia*, became a symbol of his country and made the international community aware of this little corner of Europe, then under Russian domination. He was greatly loved and honored by his fellow citizens.

Sibelius died at the age of ninety-two. In 1967 a magnificent monument was erected to his memory in Helsinki. It is a 24-ton (22-metric-ton) group of vertical metal tubes of various sizes and heights that suggest the pipes of an organ.

Present-day Finnish composers are turning out new operas and symphonies. Popular Finnish recording artists put out disks and tapes of rock music, waltzes and tangos, and music of the 1940s, 1950s, and 1960s. Hit records sell 30,000 to 100,000 copies in Finland. In relationship to the population of the country, 100,000 in Finland is equivalent to 4 million in the United States. Because the population is so small, many Finnish musicians have to go abroad to find work.

The monument to Sibelius in Helsinki

Opposite: **Composer Jean Sibelius (1865–1957) at the piano**

Rock music, imported from other countries with lyrics translated into Finnish, became popular in Finland in the 1950s and 1960s. But in the late 1970s a distinctive style known as Finnrock emerged and became popular.

The Finnish National Ballet presents programs of classical and modern dance. An annual Dance and Music Festival is held in Kuopio, the only one of its kind in Scandinavia. A few smaller dance groups can be found in Helsinki and other large towns.

People gather for recreational dancing in many places during summer. Young people like the same dances as their contemporaries all over the world. Older Finns love to dance the tango.

Theater and Movies

Dramatic arts are very popular in Finland. There are more than forty professional theater companies as well as dozens of summer, amateur, and semiprofessional theaters. The Academy of Dramatic Art in Helsinki has educational programs in both Finnish and Swedish.

Films have been produced in Finland since 1906 and talkies since 1931. Production is supported by the Finnish Film Foundation. More than a dozen feature films are produced each year on average, as well as quite a few TV movies, shorts, documentaries, and animated films. Aki Kaurismäki is Finland's most outstanding filmmaker and director.

Painting and Sculpture

The Fine Arts Society of Finland was established in 1848. The main themes of nineteenth century paintings came from

Pyynikki Summer Theater

The city of Tampere has a most unusual outdoor summer theater. Sitting on the lakeshore is a shell-shaped structure—but it isn't a bandshell or a stage. This is where the audience sits. It is filled with a bank of bleacher seats, and its floor is a turntable. Instead of using a stage with revolving parts and sets, this theater moves the audience from one viewpoint to another, using the great outdoors as its stage.

All of the forest and the lake that can be seen from the seats becomes part of the stage. Large crowds of performers can come into the scene. Some may sail up to the shore in boats, others ride into the action on horseback. It makes going to a play a real adventure.

nature. Artists of the late 1800s were largely romantics and fiercely nationalistic. Akseli Gallen-Kallela was foremost among them.

In the twentieth century, the influence of modern ideas of art—symbolism, impressionism, expressionism, surrealism—appeared in Finnish paintings. Today, illustrations, cartoons, and graphic art designs are important parts of the Finnish art scene.

Finnish sculptors work in bronze, ceramics, marble, granite, and metal. Quite a few of the nation's outstanding sculptors are women, including Eila Hiltunen, creator of the massive and awe-inspiring monument to Sibelius.

Architecture

Castles and churches that date from medieval times are lasting evidence that architecture is an old, well-established profession in Finland. Intricately carved wooden churches have survived for more than three centuries.

Before the 1900s, public buildings in Finland were designed by architects from other countries. Carl Ludwig Engel, a German, designed the neoclassic university and other buildings in Helsinki's city center in the early 1800s. He also designed several churches in other parts of Finland and drew the plans for the cathedral in Helsinki, which was completed several years after his death.

The Helsinki Railway Station, designed by Finnish architect Eliel Saarinen

Finnish architect and designer Alvar Aalto (1898–1976)

Eliel Saarinen designed the Helsinki Railway Station, before leaving Finland in 1923 for the United States. Both he and his son Eero became famous architects in America.

Alvar Aalto was a leading Finnish architect of the 1900s. His work broke away from classical designs. His modernist influence went beyond architecture to include urban planning

and interior and industrial design. One of his great works is Finlandia Hall, a conference center in Helsinki.

    Both Saarinen and Aalto were married to artists who often worked with them on projects. Loja Saarinen was a sculptor, weaver, and textile designer; Aino Marsio Aalto often completed designs from her husband's sketches.

Finlandia Hall, one of Aalto's most-striking works

Today nearly all public buildings are designed by architects who enter contests that determine who gets the contract. The resulting award-winning buildings are some of the most striking modern public structures in the world. Architectural students from many countries spend time in Finland studying the designs and techniques.

Design

Finland has a worldwide reputation in the field of modern design. The use of natural forms and materials reflects the involvement with nature that is so much a part of Finnish life and culture. Water, forests, flowers, birds, animals, and fish have inspired artists in the creation of objects that are both functional and beautiful.

Finnish designers made big names for themselves and their country in 1951. At an international art exhibition in Italy, the Milan Trienniale, Finns won more honors than artists from any other country.

Modern Finnish design is simple, graceful, and lovely. Wood is

used in modern furniture, jewelry, Christmas decorations, toys, kitchenware, and carvings. Artists create glass vases and dishes that seem to curve and flow like quiet bodies of water. Several Finnish companies have international reputations for their distinctive designs. Two examples are Marimekko textiles and Arabia dishes and ceramics.

Arabia dishes, an example of inventive Finnish design

Finnish artisans give the same attention to modern industrial design as they do to consumer goods. Art and function are both necessary elements of good design. Graduates of the University of Industrial Design create designs for telephones, computers, machinery, and many other items that are a part of everyday modern life.

Folk Art

Traditional folk arts in Finland include pottery, handblown glassware, furniture, and textiles. The best-known Finnish craft products are *ryijy* (REE-yoo) rugs. These unusual pieces of art are normally used as wall hangings. Ryijy-making combines the techniques of weaving and hand-knotting.

Physical Education

Fitness, health, and sports are linked in the minds of Finns. Surveys show that 96 percent of the people consider sports an

Soccer is one of Finland's most popular sports.

Opposite: **Matti Nykanen flies past the crowd on his way to a gold medal for ski jumping at the 1988 Olympics in Calgary, Alberta.**

important part of everyday life, and 75 percent believe Olympic competitive sports should be funded by the government. Physical education and gymnastics for both boys and girls have been included in Finnish school curriculums for at least 150 years.

Organized sports clubs thrive in every part of the country, with a total of more than a million members. Municipalities provide facilities, such as gyms, playing fields, ski slopes, skating rinks, and swimming pools.

Popular sports for schoolchildren, both girls and boys, are ice hockey and a game that is something like baseball, called *pesäpallo* (PAY-sah-pahl-loa).

Students aged fifteen to eighteen who are gifted athletes can attend one of twelve gymnasiums (sports-centered secondary schools). The gymnasiums provide a full academic curriculum plus training in competitive sports.

Winter Recreation

In a country that is covered with ice and snow for so many months, winter sports are taken for granted. Before the 1900s, skiing was unknown in many parts of the world. But in rural Finland, as in other northern European regions, skis were the only way to get from one place to another during winter.

Today, skiing is a national pastime in Finland. The school calendar includes a week-long skiing vacation. Downhill skiing, cross-country skiing, slalom racing, and ski jumping are all popular. There are more than 200 ski jumps in Finland, in small villages as well as larger towns.

On weekends, many communities sponsor organized cross-country ski trips. The largest one, the Finlandia Skiing Marathon, attracts thousands of participants. They come from many other nations as well as from all over Finland. The streets are full, ski to ski, as they set off from Hämeenlinna to Lahti, 45 miles (72 km) away.

Skating is also popular. Athletes who use the lakes for wind surfing in summer enjoy ice surfing in winter. Ice hockey is Finland's favorite spectator sport.

National Sports Heroes

During a century of Olympic Games, from 1896 to 1996, Finnish athletes took home more gold medals on a per capita basis than competitors from any other country.

In 1912 the Olympics were held in Stockholm, Sweden. Even though Finland was still under Russian control, the Finnish athletes insisted on marching and competing as a separate nation. They won twenty-six medals at that meet, nine of them gold. Hannes Kolehmainen became a national hero when he won the 5,000-meter race by a very close margin. A commentator said that he "ran Finland onto the map of the world."

Another runner, Paavo Nurmi, won nine Olympic golds and three silvers in the 1920s. A Finnish teammate, Ville Ritola, finished second to Nurmi in 1928 and went on to win five gold medals in later competitions. Lasse Viren won golds in two successive Olympics for both the 5,000- and 10,000-meter races.

The Flying Finn

Paavo Nurmi, a national sports hero, was nicknamed the Flying Finn. His statue stands in front of the Olympic Stadium in Helsinki. In addition to winning twelve Olympic medals, he set thirty-one outdoor track world records.

Nurmi lived in Turku, where he started running when he was a child. He ran through city streets with his friends. He ran alone in the woods. He ran in school competitions. His father thought running was a waste of time, but young Paavo was too independent and too competitive to be stopped.

Nurmi is remembered for his style, speed, endurance, and his amazingly long stride. He is also appreciated by Finns for the favorable publicity he brought to his young country.

Paavo Nurmi was born in 1897 and died in 1973.

Finland has also won Olympic medals in skiing, wrestling, javelin throwing, gymnastics, and canoeing. Three Finnish women athletes, Marjo Matikainen, Marja-Liisa Hämäläinen, and Marjut Lukkarinen, won gold medals for skiing in 1984, 1988, and 1992.

In 1996, at the Summer Olympics in Atlanta, Georgia, Heli Rantanen took home a gold medal in the women's javelin contest. This win brought the total golds for Finnish athletes since 1906 to 138. In addition, Finnish athletes won two silver medals and one bronze in 1996 in swimming, wrestling, and javelin.

There are no professional sports teams in Finland, but people like to watch soccer, track and field meets, ice hockey, and ski events. Finnish athletes are represented in professional ice hockey and soccer teams in other countries.

Motor sports are increasingly popular spectator events. Rally drivers Marrku Alen, Ari Vatanen, Hannu Mikkola, and Juha Kankkunen have won many world rally driving events. Finland hosted the Olympic Games in Helsinki in 1952 and the first World Athletics Championships in 1983.

Helsinki's Olympic Stadium

Pekka from Helsinki

Pekka is an eleven-year-old boy who lives in Helsinki. His father is a designer for a ceramics manufacturer, his mother teaches school. Pekka has a younger sister, Anja.

It is the first day of July, and the children wake up very early. Today is the day the whole family moves to their summer cottage on a small lake near Tampere. They have been going to the cottage on weekends for a month, but now they'll stay there for most of the summer. Both parents will be on vacation for six weeks.

Vacationing Finns enjoy a traditional crayfish dinner.

Pekka looks forward to hiking, swimming, and playing with his sister and parents. This is the kind of summer he has spent ever since he can remember. The family will spend much time in the forests, picking mushrooms and blueberries. Anyone may pick these delicacies on public lands.

Pekka's mother makes wonderful blueberry juice, which she sometimes mixes with other wild berries. If the berries are plentiful this year, she will can or freeze as many as possible, to use later in pancakes and pies.

On Saturday nights, and several times during the week, the family will go to their sauna. The small, prefabricated wooden building under the trees and close to the cottage is a favorite spot for telling stories and jokes to each other. Pekka loves to jump into the cold lake after a spell in the sauna.

The cottage is quite new. It is not right on the lakeshore, because laws have been passed to protect the lakes from pollution. New homes have to be a certain distance away from the water.

A preschool in Espoo

Education

Pekka, like most Finnish children who live in cities and towns, went to preschool from age five to seven. Formal education starts when children are seven. Schools are free, and compulsory for all children between seven and sixteen years of age. Books, hot lunches, dental care, and transportation to school are also free. Children who live far away from any school receive a lodging allowance.

Basic education in elementary schools has been a strong tradition for over a century in Finland. The importance of literacy was recognized centuries before, when the Protestant Church leaders stressed reading in order to encourage ordinary people to read the Bible. The church law requiring proof that people could read before they were permitted to marry was very effective. Finland has one of the highest literacy rates in the world.

Opposite: **A group of students at a library in the Åland Islands**

Swedish-speaking Finns are guaranteed schooling in their own tongue; there are Swedish schools and universities. Smaller ethnic minorities, such as the Sami, however, are constantly fighting for recognition of their language and culture in educational institutions.

Increased emphasis has been placed on higher education since the 1950s, as a means of helping national economic growth. The aim is to make secondary-level education available to everyone. Schools are almost 100 percent owned and financed by society. Most secondary-level schools are owned by local municipalities and partially financed by the state. All universities and other institutions of higher learning are owned by the state. Finnish education, though locally run, is highly centralized with a good many directives and regulations from the state.

Secondary-level education is divided into vocational and general schools. Students who graduate from an academic, or general, school must take an exam to qualify for further education.

Vocational schools have fifteen branches of study that take from two to four years. Courses that lead to manual work are called school-level. Those that train more highly skilled workers and managers are called institute-level.

Orienteering

A favorite hobby among Finns of all ages is orienteering. It is a game, but it also teaches the useful skills needed avoid getting lost, either in a city or in the woods.

By the time they are in high school, most young people have become very good at orienteering. They've been taken many times to a remote location, given a compass and map or minimal directions, and left to find their way back to a meeting place. The activity continues into adulthood. Sports clubs sponsor orienteering treks of varying levels of difficulty.

Children begin to learn these skills in the early grades. They are taught about directions and how to use maps. Then they are taken to a certain spot in the playground or near the school and left to find their way back. They are watched by supervisors, of course, so they can't get into real trouble. But they do learn how to take care of themselves.

Women's Rights

The concept of women's rights is not new in Finland, the first European nation to give women the right to vote and run for public office. Normally, several cabinet positions as well as a third or more of the seats in the parliament are held by women. Women are active members and leaders in labor unions.

While full equality has not yet been achieved, a 1988 study found that Finland ranked just behind Sweden and ahead of the United States as one of the best places in the world for women to live. This conclusion was based on health, educational, economic, and legal factors that affect women.

About three-fourths of the women in Finland hold jobs outside the home. They make up nearly half of Finland's workforce. Women have equal rights with men in child-custody matters, including choosing their child's legal nationality and surname. National laws forbid any discrimination on the basis of sex.

Despite these gains, the level of education they have achieved, and the strong feminist tradition in Finland, women are still paid, on average, only about two-thirds as much as their male coworkers. They hold far fewer supervisory, managerial, and decision-making positions. Also, the day-care system is not yet as comprehensive and widespread as it must become if women are to have full equality.

There is tremendous competition for openings in the universities. Only about half of those who take the entrance exam pass it, and there is space for fewer than one out of four of those who pass. Students complain that university selection policies result in admission based on social and regional inequalities rather than on individual ability.

Finland has seventeen universities and ten upper-level specialty schools, including three art schools. Only the University of Helsinki existed before the 1900s. About 90,000 students are enrolled in post-secondary education. More than half of them get some kind of student aid through study grants or low-interest loans. Slightly over half of the university students are women.

Computer training for students in Finland is nearly universal. Finland has more people per capita who use Internet services than any other country in the world except Iceland.

Teenagers in Finland

Internationalization

During the 1940s and 1950s, the Finns were so busy with reconstruction and industrialization they had few contacts with the outside world. By the 1960s, television sets had become common in many living rooms and Finns began to watch programs beamed in from several other countries. They started to join other tourists in flying south to warmer climates for vacations. Interest in foreign affairs and cultures grew, especially among young people.

A well-educated young person in 1950 had probably not visited any other country except possibly Sweden. He or she could speak Swedish and a little German but probably socialized almost exclusively with other Finns.

Today's Finnish-speaking students start learning English in the third grade. (Meanwhile, Swedish-speaking pupils study Finnish.) By their late teens, many Finnish-speaking university students have picked up Swedish and German, plus a smattering of French. Many of them have spent a summer or two working in Germany or another European country, and most have taken long railroad trips through western Europe. They have made friends with students from other countries and may be active in international student organizations.

Opportunities are increasing for Finnish students to work and study abroad, as well as for exchange students to come to Finland.

Adult Education

Nearly a million Finns are enrolled in some form of continuing education each year. Some are taking courses related to their careers. Others are catching up on secondary education through evening schools, broadening their horizons through special institutes and study centers, or learning new skills at vocational centers. Study grants are available for adults over thirty who have been working full-time for at least five years.

A uniquely Nordic tradition is the folk high school. Common throughout Scandinavia, this kind of school originated in Denmark in the 1800s. Adults stay at folk institutes and folk academies for several weeks and take a variety of subjects from handicrafts to economics and international policy.

Food

Traditional Finnish foods are hearty and heavy in calories. Vegetables are apt to be expensive. Staples are meat, fish, potatoes, dairy products, and baked goods made of rye, wheat, barley, or oats. This kind of diet was essential for people who made their living by hard manual labor. Lumberjacks, fishermen, and farmers needed a lot of calories to get through a day of hard work.

However, eating habits have changed as more people live in cities and work at less strenuous jobs. And just as in many

A typical Finnish meal includes fish and potatoes.

Two Kinds of Bread

At the end of World War II, several hundred thousand Karelians left their homes in eastern Finland because the Russians had taken over their land. The Finnish government helped them establish new homesteads, and many of them found temporary homes with other Finnish families.

Even though both groups were true Finns, they had a few different customs and tastes that sometimes led to arguments. The Karelians were used to making fresh bread every day or two. Some of the western Finns were fond of *reikäleipä* (RAY-kah-lei-pah) or "bread with a hole." The dough was shaped into round, flat loaves with a hole in the middle. Housewives would bake many loaves at a time, run a long spindle like a broom handle through the holes, hang them up, and keep them for weeks. The westerners enjoyed the hard bread.

A story is told that one western woman complained to her Karelian housemate, "You bake so often you're going to break my oven." The reply was, "Your bread is so hard it's going to break our teeth."

other countries, fast foods have become popular. Pizza, hamburgers, and kabobs can be found in most urban areas.

Finnish foods have also been influenced by their next-door neighbors, Russia and Sweden. Eastern Finns eat a lot of *borscht* (a hearty soup from Russia) and pastries filled with fish. Westerners like to start a meal with a buffet table called a smorgasbord like those found in Sweden and other Scandinavian countries.

Traditional foods appear on holidays. Special buns filled with almond paste and whipped cream, *laskiais-pulla* (LAHSS-kee-ahis-pool-lah), are served on Shrove Tuesday. Typical Lenten meals are pea soup and pigs' feet. Easter is time for a special cheesecake called *pasha* (PAH-shah) made in a mold that decorates the cake with Easter symbols.

May Day is the time to celebrate the end of the long, dark, northern winter, even though there may be more sleet and snow to come. It is time for some *sima* (SIM-ah), a sparkling lemon drink, served with a fried cruller—*tippaleipä* (TIP-pah-lay-pah).

Midsummer, when the sun barely sets at all, is celebrated with pancakes and sausages grilled outdoors. Soon, berries and mushrooms are in season. Finns use these delicacies in many soups, sauces, desserts, and other dishes.

Favorite Christmas or *joulu* (YOA-loo) dishes are ham with prunes or *joulukinkku* (YOA-loo-kingk-koo), rye bread or *joululimppu* (YOA-loo-limp-poo), and prune turnovers or *joulutortut* (YOA-loo-toa-ret-toot).

The Finns make many good cheeses. One, often homemade, is called *leipäjuusto* (LAY-pae-yooss-toa) or "squeaky cheese." It is used in various dishes, sometimes baked with cream and berries or cubed into beef stew.

A traditional Christmas or *joulu* dinner

Breakfast in a country home may be quite a filling meal, with oatmeal followed by an open-faced sandwich of meat, cheese, cucumbers, and tomatoes. The main meal of the day is usually eaten at noon. The entrée is often a meat or fish stew, meatballs, stuffed cabbage leaves, or a casserole. A lighter meal may be soup or salad, along with pastries stuffed with rice, farina, or potatoes. Favorite desserts are creamy baked rice pudding called *riisipuuro* (REE-si-poo-roa), cheese torte made with fresh blueberries called *mustikkarahkatorttu* (MOOSS-tik-kahr-ah-kah-toar-too), and ice cream.

Johan Ludvig Runeberg

Finns commemorate the birthday of their national poet, Johan Ludvig Runeberg, each February 5, another holiday that has a special food associated with it. "Runeberg cakes" are sold in all the shops.

Born in 1804, Runeberg wrote poetry about love and nature, as well as idealism and military heroics. His best known work, *Tales of the Ensign Stål*, is greatly admired as a classic of Scandinavian literature. The words to the Finnish national anthem came from this book.

A statue of Runeberg, sculpted by his son Walter in 1885, stands in Esplanade Park in Helsinki. The female figure on the pedestal is the patron muse of Finnish poetry.

Finns drink a lot of coffee, *kahvi* (KAH-vi)—as much as nine cups a day, according to some sources. It is often served with *pulla* (POOL-lah), a yeast bread flavored with cardamom and almonds.

Coffee, or *kahvi*, is often served with a treat.

Social Welfare

Finland has one of the most advanced welfare systems in the world. In fact, true poverty has nearly disappeared.

Taxes and the cost of living are high compared to some other developed countries. However, Finnish people are assured through government programs of having basic necessities and decent living conditions. This applies to everyone, from infants to the elderly, whether or not they are able to work. The benefits of social legislation are believed to be a citizen's basic right, not just a handout for less fortunate people.

Family allowances and benefits start with birth. The mother of a new baby receives a cash maternity benefit, and one or both parents are entitled to a daily allowance while on leave of absence from their jobs until the infant is nine months old. If necessary, a parent can get a leave of absence to take care of children up to three years of age or can work shorter hours. In either case, they receive an allowance.

Although a Finnish day-care system is not yet fully in place, in theory, families are entitled to day care for children up to age six and after-school care up to age ten for children of working parents. Families also receive a basic allowance for each child under the age of seventeen. The state assures a minimum income for everyone through insurance and pension plans, as well as various special services for the elderly.

Health Insurance

Finland's aim is to ensure equality in health care for all. Prevention of disease is emphasized.

The national health insurance program covers everyone living in Finland. Medical, laboratory, X-ray, and hospital services, as well as necessary travel for services, are covered. Patients pay a small amount and the government takes care of the rest. Dental care is provided for people born after 1956 and for veterans. Sickness insurance pays an allowance to compensate for lost wages due to illness or accident.

Much of Finland's primary health care is handled by local health centers. Children get regular medical checkups, inoculations, and first-aid services at these centers and through their schools. There are about 430 hospitals in the country. A few are privately run; the rest are maintained by local authorities with funds supplemented by the government.

Disabled persons receive the same services as the rest of the population, in addition to special services where needed. These include housing, transport, sheltered work, education, training, and interpretation for the hearing-impaired. As evidence of the success of the health system, Finland points with pride to its low infant mortality and high life-expectancy rates.

Many programs support Finland's elderly.

What, Then, Is Finland?

It is a gateway to the Arctic, a bridge between East and West. It is majestic forests and glassy lakes, huge icebreakers plowing through a frozen sea. It is a nation of people who think for themselves and believe in helping one another. It is the soaring music of Jean Sibelius, the courage and determination of Paavo Nurmi. It is the magic of the *Kalevala*, the innocence and goodwill of the Moomins. And much more.

It is *Suomi*, Finland.

Timeline

c. 2500 B.C.	Egyptians build the Pyramids and Sphinx in Giza.
563 B.C.	Buddha is born in India.
A.D. 313	The Roman emperor Constantine recognizes Christianity.
610	The prophet Muhammad begins preaching a new religion called Islam.
1054	The Eastern (Orthodox) and Western (Roman) Churches break apart.
1066	William the Conqueror defeats the English in the Battle of Hastings.
1095	Pope Urban II proclaims the First Crusade.
1215	King John seals the Magna Carta.
1300s	The Renaissance begins in Italy.
1347	The Black Death sweeps through Europe.
1453	Ottoman Turks capture Constantinople, conquering the Byzantine Empire.
1492	Columbus arrives in North America.
1500s	The Reformation leads to the birth of Protestantism.
1776	The Declaration of Independence is signed.
1789	The French Revolution begins.

Finnish History

Finland becomes part of the kingdom of Sweden.	1155
A treaty between Sweden and Russia divides Karelia.	1323
Sweden-Finland breaks free from Denmark under King Gustav I Vasa.	1523
Mikael Agricola, Bishop of Turku, translates the Bible into Finnish.	1548

Finnish History

Sweden surrenders Finland to Russia and the country becomes a partly self-ruling Grand Duchy under Czar Alexander I.	1809
Composer Jean Sibelius is born.	1865
Finland adopts universal suffrage and becomes the first European country to give women the vote.	1906
Finland declares independence from Russia on December 6.	1917
Republican constitution is adopted and Kaarlo Juho Ståhlberg becomes Finland's first president.	1919
The Soviet Union defeats Finland in the Winter War.	1939–1940
The Soviet Union defeats Finland in the Continuation War.	1941–1944
Finland makes separate peace with the Allies and establishes a policy of international neutrality.	1944
Olympics are held in Helsinki.	1952
Finland joins the United Nations.	1955
Urho Kaleva Kekkonen is elected president.	1956
The Helsinki Accord is signed.	1975
Finland becomes the fifteenth nation to join the European Union.	1995

World History

1865	The American Civil War ends.
1914	World War I breaks out.
1917	The Bolshevik Revolution brings Communism to Russia.
1929	Worldwide economic depression begins.
1939	World War II begins, following the German invasion of Poland.
1957	The Vietnam War starts.
1989	The Berlin Wall is torn down, as Communism crumbles in Eastern Europe.
1996	Bill Clinton reelected U.S. president.

Fast Facts

Official name: Republic of Finland (*Suomi* in Finnish)

Helsinki

Capital: Helsinki

Official languages: Finnish and Swedish

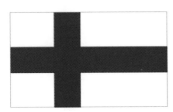

Flag of Finland

President Martti Ahtisaari

Official religion: None

National anthem: "Maamme" in Finnish or "Vart Land" in Swedish, meaning "our land" (The national anthem was composed by Fredrik Pacius and written by J. L. Runeberg.)

Government: Multiparty republic with one legislative house

Chief of state: President

Head of government: Prime minister

Area and dimensions: The country covers 130,568 square miles (338,145 sq km), making Finland the seventh largest country in Europe. Finland stretches 717 miles (1,154 km) north to south and 336 miles (541 km) east to west.

Bordering countries: Finland is bordered by Norway on the north, Russia on the east, the Baltic Sea on the south and the southwest, and Sweden on the northwest.

Highest elevation: Mount Haltia, 4,356 feet (1,328 m)

Lowest elevation: Sea level

Average temperatures:

	in June	in December
Helsinki:	63°F (17°C)	21°F (-6°C)
Lapland:	55°F (13°C)	1°F (-17°C)

Average annual rainfall:

Helsinki	24.5 inches (62.2 cm)
Mariehamn	21 inches (53.5 cm)
Joensuu	23.9 inches (60.6 cm)
Oulu	18.6 inches (47.4 cm)
Usjok	15.7 inches (40 cm)

National population: (1995)	5,117,000	
Populations of largest cities in Finland:	Helsinki	525,031
	Espoo	191,247
	Tampere	182,742
	Vantaa	166,480
	Turku	164,744

Famous landmarks: Helsinki enthralls visitors with its magnificent buildings and churches, zoo, theme park, and other urban attractions. Outside the capital, landmarks include the medieval castle and cathedral in Turku, the historic cathedrals of Porvoo, the wooden buildings of Old Rauma, and the seaside views of Mariehamn. Two of the best-known points of interest in the Lake District are Punkaharju ridge, formed during the Ice Age, and the Orthodox monastery and convent at Heinavesi.

Turku Castle

Industry: Nearly 40 percent of Finland's exports come from the metal and engineering industry. Finnish companies are active in research, development, and the use of modern automation and industrial robots. Finland ranks second in the world, after Canada, in paper exports (pulp, paperboard, plywood, and particle board). Finnish experts also design machinery for manufacturers throughout the world.

Currency: The markka, known outside Finland as the Finnmark (FIM), is issued in denominations of 10, 20, 50, 100, 500, and 1,000. One markka equals 100 pennis. Coins come in 10 and 50 pennis and in 1,5, and 10 markkas. 1997 exchange rate: U.S.$1 = 4.6 FIM

Weights and measures:	Metric system
Literacy:	Virtually 100%

Common Finnish words and phrases:		
	anteeksi	excuse me
	ei	no
	hei or *terve*	hello
	huomenta	good morning
	hyvaa iltaa	good evening
	kiitos	thank you
	Kiitos hyvää.	I'm fine, thanks.
	kyllä	yes
	Mikä sinun nimi on?	What is your name?
	Mistä olet kotoisin?	Where are you from?
	Mitä kuuluu?	How are you?
	näkemiin	good-bye
	Ole hyva.	You're welcome.
	Puhutteko englantia?	Do you speak English?

(Pronunciation is mostly phonetic. The stress always falls on the first syllable.)

To Find Out More

Nonfiction

▶ Brownstone and Franck, ed. *The Scandinavian-American Heritage*. New York: Facts On File, 1988.

▶ Garrett, Dan. *Scandinavia*. Chatham, NJ: Raintree Steck-Vaughn, 1991.

▶ Lander, Patricia S., and Claudette Charbonneau. *The Land and People of Finland*. New York: J. B. Lippincott, 1990.

▶ Lerner Geography Department Staff. *Finland in Pictures*. Minneapolis: Lerner Publications, 1991.

▶ Reynolds, J. *Far North: Vanishing Cultures*. New York: Harcourt Brace, 1992.

▶ Vitebsky, Piers. *Saami of Lapland*. New York: Thomson Learning, 1994.

Fiction

▶ Jansson, Tove. *Moominsummer Madness*. New York: Farrar, Straus and Giroux, 1991.

▶ Kingman, Lee. *The Meeting Post: A Story of Lapland*. New York: Thomas Y. Crowell, 1972.

▶ McNeil, M. E. *The Magic Storysinger: From the Finnish Epic Kalevala*. Owings Mills, MD: Stemmer House, 1993.

Folklore

▶ Jones, Gwyn, retold by. *Scandinavian Legends and Folk-Tales*. New York: Oxford University Press, 1992.

▶ Troughton, Joanna, retold by. *The Magic Mill: A Finnish Folk Tale from the Kalevala*. New York: Peter Bedrick, 1989.

Reference

▶ Federal Research Division, Library of Congress. *Finland: A Country Study*. Lanham, MD: Bernam Press, 1990.

▶ Rakjanen, Aini. *Of Finnish Ways*. New York: Harper & Rowe, 1984.

▶ Taylor-Wilkie, Doreen, ed. *Finland*. Boston: Houghton Mifflin, 1995.

Videotapes

▶ *Finland: A Song of Summer*. New York: Finnish Tourist Board.

▶ *Scandinavia*. Columbia, SC: South Carolina ETV.

Websites

▶ **Embassy of Finland**
http://www.finland.org
Provides comprehensive information about Finland, including the country's latest news and travel opportunities. Includes information about Sami history and culture.

▶ **Finnish Government**
http://www.vn.fi
Lists information about Finland's ministers, president, and parliament.

▶ **Finnish Trade Network**
http://www.tradepoint.fi
Reports the business and economic news of Finland.

▶ Sibelius Academy
http://www.siba.fi/welcome-eng.html
Provides links to a wide variety of music pages from Finnish folk to rock and pop to jazz and blues pages.
(The site is run by Finland's only music university.)

▶ Kalevala
http://www.vn.fi/vn/um/finfo/english/kalevala.html
Provides excerpts of the Kalevala in translation with explanation and biographical information about the author.

Organizations and Embassies

▶ **Embassy of Finland**
3301 Massachusetts Avenue NW
Washington, DC 20008
(202) 298-5800
info@finland.org

▶ **Consulate General of Finland**
866 UN Plaza, Suite 250
New York, NY 10017
(212) 750-4400
finconny@ix.netcom.com

▶ **Finland Trade Center**
866 UN Plaza, Suite 249
New York, NY 10017
(212) 750-4411
ftcny@ix.netcom.com

▶ **The Finnish American Chamber of Commerce**
866 UN Plaza, Suite 249
New York, NY 10017
(212) 821-0225

Index

Page numbers in *italics* indicate illustrations

Meet the Author

SYLVIA McNAIR was born in Korea and believes she inherited a love of travel from her missionary parents. She grew up in Vermont, where "the climate and people are actually a lot like Finland's," she says. After graduating from Oberlin College in Ohio, she held a variety of jobs, married, had four children, and settled in the Chicago area. She now lives in Evanston, Illinois. She is the author of several travel guides and a dozen books for young people published by Children's Press.

"The first step to writing a book is to head to the library. When writing about a country, I send for any relevant materials published by the U.S. government and pick up some guidebooks and a dictionary of the country's language from the bookstore. I use my computer to search for some kinds of information on the Internet.

"Next I make contact, in person if possible, with the country's tourist office, embassy, and consulate. I ask a lot of questions and get all the printed material from these officials I can.

"If I can find people from that nation living in my area, I arrange to interview them. Graduate students who are studying in this country are always a great source—and fun to get to know. For this book, I was able to attend Finnfest '96, an annual gathering of Finnish descendants who live in the United States and Canada to celebrate their heritage. I attended several lectures, ate Finnish food, talked with people, and bought more books.

"Then I took a short trip to Finland, something I don't always have the chance to do. Seeing the cities and countryside and talking with people who live there brings everything alive for me.

"Last (although I've been working on it all along) comes the writing part. I sit at my computer for several hours each day and print out many drafts before I'm satisfied. And while I'm writing, I'm imagining that I am visiting that country again, maybe even that I'm living there. Writing about places is almost as great an adventure as visiting them."

Photo Credits